The New Oil

Using Innovative Business Models

to Turn Data Into Profit

Arent van 't Spijker

Technics Publications

Published by:
Technics Publications, LLC
2 Lindsley Road
Basking Ridge, NJ 07920 USA
http://www.TechnicsPub.com

First Printing 2014

Copyright © 2014 by Arent van 't Spijker

ISBN: 978-1-935504-82-5

Library of Congress Control Number: 2014939223

To Angelina

Table of Contents

Part I: Shift Happens

Part II: The Value of Data

Part III: Patterns in Practice

Acknowledgements

The concepts presented in this book are not simply my own. They have been inspired by the authors whose books I have read. By the family, friends and colleagues that I have had so many conversations with. And not in the least by the customers who asked me to help them leverage the value of their data. I would like to thank each and every person who has challenged my ideas and convictions during those situations. And of course my gratitude goes out to all the people that have participated in the many interviews and business cases that are mentioned in the book. They form the essence of this book. In particular I want to thank my wife, Angelina, for her motivation, support and reflection. And Ralph Hofman for his work on the Business Model Canvas patterns, Jan Bakker and Stefan Bollars for their review and constructive criticism on the material and Charlotte Jongejan for her corrections and linguistic support. My special thanks go to Cor Nagtegaal and Ed Peelen, whose reviews, insights and guidance provided me with much needed structure and direction.

I am most grateful.

Arent van 't Spijker

1 - Introduction

In a speech held in 2012, Neelie Kroes, vice president of the European Commission and responsible for the Digital Agenda, referred to data as 'the new oil'. Kroes was not the first to coin the phrase: Clive Humby, founder of UK–based customer insights company Dunhumby was, arguably, the first when he mentioned the analogy six years earlier. His interpretation of data as oil focused on the idea that data needs to be 'drilled down' and 'refined', after which it becomes valuable and can 'power decision making'. Neelie Kroes was one of the first people to refer to data as 'the new oil' from the perspective of an entire economy. Oil changed our world and economy by driving the development of the internal combustion engine, central heating and plastics. Oil, as a technology, fueled an economic force that inexorably changed the way people lived and worked.

Today, data is fueling a very similar change. It impacts not just high-tech, high-profile companies, but also old-school, low-tech industries all around the world. This book will show you how data is changing the traditional business paradigm, becoming the dominant factor in how products generate added value. The clear distinction between data as a byproduct of a production process or as the raw material of a new product is fading. Data is increasingly becoming the core value of a product, up to the point where it is not always clear whether the product is valued for its intrinsic features or for its ability to process or generate data.

The New Oil clearly shows that companies in many industries are shifting towards a data-driven strategy: electronics manufacturers are changing focus from hardware to customer platforms, utilities are shifting from energy production to leveraging data from smart meters, and banks are moving from providing transaction services to analyzing spending patterns. Throughout the book, many examples highlight the potential for Data Driven Strategy.

The New Oil is split into three parts. The first part shows how societal and technological changes have turned businesses and individuals into new data consumers and data into a valuable asset. The second part shows how various business models allow organizations to best leverage the value that data creates in these new markets. The third part explains how successful companies put these business models to practice and combine new data driven ventures with their existing business.

Neelie Kroes' view on the potential of data is one of opportunity, inspiration and drive. That is exactly what this book is about. It outlines the opportunity of data for your organization; it aims to inspire you to find your specific opportunities and to drive your creativity to innovate and find new markets and customers.

PART I

SHIFT HAPPENS

2 - The Value of Data

How a minimalistic approach made Google the biggest company in the world

In 1995, the Digital Equipment Corporation (DEC) launched a new website that caused more than a stir in the still-infant Internet community. The website offered a new, powerful search engine for the World Wide Web. That in itself was not particularly striking. The emerging search engine battlefield was firmly dominated by Lycos and Yahoo! (both founded in 1994, the birth year of the web) but constantly under threat by new entrants vying for position in the almost liquid market for Internet dominance. What set this website apart was the lack of content on its homepage; it contained nothing more than a small input field for users to type the subject of their query. AltaVista, as the site was called, would come to be the blueprint for query-based search engines to follow. In a way, it defined the principles for the rival it would be defeated by only a few years later: Google.

Users loved AltaVista from the start. The searches returned results that were easy to interpret and relevant. But more important for its success was the speed at which it operated. In those early days, the Internet was a tenuously slow environment, where people depended on analog lines to transfer data at speeds of 28.8 Kbps (over 500 times slower than today) if they were lucky. Web pages could take up to a minute to load, and receiving incorrect or irrelevant results from a search query was the cause of frequent frustration. AltaVista changed that.

AltaVista hosted an impressive array of servers to carry out search requests as quickly as possible. In fact, AltaVista started out as something of a muscle flexing exercise by DEC to prove to the world (and competitors) that their servers were the fastest machines around. To optimize the entire speed chain, all unnecessary data was removed from the search page, allowing it to load results as quickly as possible onto users' computer screens. No colors, no text, no images; just an input field and a 'Go' button. This minimalistic interface reduced page loading time by tens of seconds. It also meant the omission of the traditional banner advertisements, which were at that time standard practice on virtually all commercial websites. This meant no income for DEC, but as AltaVista served a marketing purpose rather than a commercial one, it was not considered a problem at that time.

Between 1996 and 1998, AltaVista topped the search engine charts in the Internet, and during that time the standard for search engine user interfaces was set. It survives to this day. In 1998 a sequence of events led to the rapid demise of AltaVista's dominance. DEC was sold to Compaq, a company far less intent on showing off its search capability. It is safe to assume that the search engine, hardly the core business for either party in this takeover, did not get the attention it required, especially as a serious new competitor had opened up shop. Two Stanford students, Sergey Brin and Larry Page, had improved the basic principles of Internet searches by adding a set of complex mathematical algorithms ranking search results according to relevance. PageRank, as the algorithm was called, was a huge improvement over the existing search mechanisms and formed the key product of their technology startup: Google. But whilst improving the engine, Brin and Page did not touch the successful simplicity of the interface. AltaVista had defined the de facto interface for search pages, and Google stuck to it. Arguably that was one of the most dramatic commercial decisions in history, since it paved the way for the commercial driver behind Google and one of the most prolific examples of Data Driven Strategy: the AdWords advertising system.

During the first years of dramatic success, Google financed its rapid growth primarily through venture capital. Even though this was at the height of the dot-com bubble and investors' money seemed abundant, Google management realized it was in drastic need of an income model scalable to the use of the system. Banner advertisements were an unlikely candidate for success. This was due to the fact that Google's pages were visited so often that the supply of banner advertisements simply could not meet the demand of search result pages. In other words, there was a shortage of advertisers capable of serving up sufficient ads to scale the business model. By the year 2000, Google had built up considerable experience in placing sponsored links at the top of results pages. These advertisements looked like regular search results, but advertisers in fact paid to have their results shown at the top of the results page. Google had confronted and overcome users' resistance to the display of commercial search results. Now the company had to overcome the same problem as before: a lack of advertisers to service the millions of pages the site served every day. And banners and other graphically intruding ad forms were a no-go area.

The answer was found in a system called AdWords, which was launched in the year 2000. AdWords is a self-service system based on the principle that everybody should be able to place small ads on Google result pages, only paying for clicks per ad. The system quite elegantly solved two of Google's substantial business problems. Firstly, by supplying the huge amount of advertisers needed to fill the ad-space it generates on its search result pages, and secondly by providing an efficient way to collect income from thousands of (small budget) advertisers without them having to commit to a host of advertising intermediaries or agencies.

The AdWords system allows anyone to design a simple text-based advertisement and enables them to indicate which search terms are relevant to their advertisement. For instance, our advertiser is the owner of a small hotel in Berlin. The relevant search terms he would likely choose will include 'Berlin' and 'Hotel', but he might also choose to link his ad to search results for one of Berlin's highlights, the 'Brandenburger Tor'. The idea behind this being that the ad will be shown on Google result pages for searches on that particular word. An automated system subsequently determines the monetary value for each of these search terms. It does so by calculating factors such as the frequency this word has been searched over the last few days and how many other advertisers are using the search term to place ads. The advertiser will then set a maximum amount he wants to spend per month and adds his credit card data. Once the system is up and running, it automatically serves the ads to relevant search result pages. Each time a user clicks the ad, the cost is deducted from the monthly maximum amount, and after that amount has run out, no more ads will be placed. At the end of the month, the advertiser's credit card will be billed for the agreed maximum amount. This system benefits both user and provider; the advertiser only pays for advertisements that were actually clicked by users, and Google has a fully automated money making machine which is endlessly scalable to the increasing volume of search result pages served. The system is so successful that for 2011, Google reported an advertising income of over US$36 billion, most of which was served by the AdWords system.[1]

It was not one dramatic commercial decision but a culmination of events that led to Google's new commercial strategy and billions of dollars in revenue. The combination of the minimal interface of AltaVista and the absence of immediate necessity to make money from banner advertising created an environment where, much later, AdWords could be launched successfully. Had Google started selling graphically attractive and interactive banner advertisements as early as 1998, creating a fertile ground for the minimalistic (but far more scalable) AdWords text ads would likely have been difficult.

The success of AdWords was near immediate. Tens of thousands of small and medium-sized enterprises around the world found in AdWords a simple, cheap and highly effective way to advertise on the Internet without large advertising budgets or involving an ad agency. Now anyone could advertise on the world's largest search engine and achieve measurable and effective results. The system snowballed. Google management discovered it could potentially serve more ads than it served search result pages. To maximize revenues Google could opt to increase prices per ad, but this would make it less attractive for users to participate and eventually hollow out the system. What Google needed was not more advertisers, but more pages to place ads.

The driving success of AdWords lies in the fact that the ads are always placed in a context that is relevant to the reader. If the reader enters a search query in Google for a hotel in Berlin, the search results page will display advertisements that are aimed at people looking for a combination of 'hotel' and 'Berlin'. The ads may be served from Hilton Hotels but equally likely from the small hotel owner we used in our example before. To the reader, the ads are relevant and therefore no more (or less) intrusive than traditional ads. They are instead perceived as valuable content.

In a brilliant example of scaling opportunities, Google expanded the AdWords system so that website owners could create a space on their pages to display Google Ads. In exchange for ad placement, the website owners received money from Google for each click on an ad that was shown on their website. This system provided Google with millions of additional pages to place ads. By using its existing search technology, Google was able to 'scan' pages before placing ads, guaranteeing that the ads were relevant to the website content. This way, the advertisement of our Berlin hotel owner could be placed on a Google search results page about Berlin as well as on a website about the cultural highlights of the city that was created by a fellow townsman.

In practice, and I presume without much careful planning, the introduction of AdWords changed the business model of Google by adding a target group to its clientele that did not use Google for its excellent search product but for its excellent search audience. Google was no longer merely a provider of an effective search engine financed by placing ads next to search results. It was now the provider of an excellent advertising platform powered (and monetized) in the context of a search engine. From that perspective, Google was no longer limited to providing the best search engine; it was challenged to provide additional services to leverage the advertising platform.

Most businesses scale up by improving on or expanding their existing product or service. For Google that would have meant expanding its search engine service by serving more search results and generating more revenue with search-related ads. It could, for instance, have ventured into specific search solutions for second-hand cars or for cheap airline tickets. But Google chose not to do this. Through AdWords, Google's business model had changed from search focused to advertisement focused. Google's business is dependent on an environment where ads can be placed rather than merely a search engine that draws in sufficient users to make it attractive for advertisers. This may seem a simple nuance of definition, but the difference could not be more significant. Google's initial business model uses the information (search term) generated by a product (search engine) to generate revenue. In this new business model, Google uses various products to generate information (search terms and other context) that it can subsequently sell to customers (advertisers).

As Google has searched for more products to generate context, they have made some interesting choices. One of the first big steps away from the search-related business came with the introduction of Gmail, Google's free e-mail service. Gmail caused quite a stir as it became clear that Google placed advertisements on the e-mail pages of users. That fact in itself was not overly shocking. However, these advertisements were related to the context of the messages received and sent, meaning that Google systems apparently analyzed the contents of e-mails before placing the relevant advertisement on that same page. Not everybody was enthusiastic about Google systems 'reading' their e-mail. However, the controversy did not hinder Gmail's success, and since then Gmail has become one of the most widely used web based e-mail systems, serving millions of pages to users daily. Each page of Gmail content containing ads and generating a constant revenue stream for Google. In a similar fashion, Google launched Google Maps, a geographical information system providing street maps and satellite imagery from almost anywhere in the world. Again, the service was accompanied by small textual ads.

AdWords changed Google's business paradigm. It took a secondary product from Google's search service—context information—and turned it into the backbone of the company's profitability. It turned Google into a service provider offering products including a video upload website (YouTube), the dominant competitor of Microsoft in office software (Google Apps), the manufacturer of groundbreaking digital glasses (Google Glass), the world's leading smartphone operating system (Android) and even the creator of the driverless car.

Google was one of the first non-publishing corporations to recognize and acknowledge the value of data as a core product rather than a byproduct. It was the first company to develop and launch products made not for their direct sales value but for their ability to generate information, with the aim to monetize that data. More and more, companies are following in

Google's footsteps. Companies like Getty Images, a stock photography publisher that provides free access to images it previously sold and now makes money from analytics and in-image advertising. Or Nike, which monetizes the data from its Nike+ products. Throughout this book I will show why these developments in our markets are happening today, how organizations of all shapes and sizes build effective business models for Data Driven Strategy and how they put their ideas to practice.

3 - Change Happens

How data is already making a big impact on your daily life and work

In his book *The World Is Flat*, Pulitzer Prize winner Thomas Friedman discusses how the world has seen three eras of globalization.[2] Globalization 1.0 began when Columbus discovered America, changing European rules on their position in the world and the way they discovered and colonized it. Globalization 2.0 lasted from around 1800 to 2000 with multinationals as the driving force, from Dutch-English joint-stock companies to the hype of the dot-com startups. Globalization 3.0 is where we are today. It is characterized by what Friedman calls the 'flat-world platform', where individuals and small groups are empowered by personal computers, fiber-optic networks and collaboration tools. Unlike Globalization 1.0 and 2.0, in Globalization 3.0 there are no institutions that drive change. The ability to move without an institution is driving it. No single government or company sets off change; rather, it is the easy ability to communicate, the willingness of people to share information and participate in networks or the fact that we have become highly mobile.

In the first chapter of this book, I described how Google changed its business model by monetizing the data that originated from its primary processes. And even though Google paved the way for many changes, it could not have been successful without a customer base that was ready for its offering. Social, economic and technological changes have made it possible for companies to adopt new technologies and business models that in turn influenced our society, economy and technology. Increasingly, companies are changing their business models to successfully monetize their data. Driving this focus on data is not simply the current technological capability. It is a combination of changes in people, technology and economic principles that cause Friedman's Globalization 3.0.

In the following two chapters I will show examples of how information is actually changing our world in a fundamental way, resulting in the flat world Friedman describes. You will learn how consecutive generations use and value information in a different way and how the current generation drives a whole new way of valuing data. I will show how business value is shifting from content—which was, not so long ago, still the driving force for value—to platforms that do not control the content but derive value from the analysis of who is using it. I will demonstrate how many traditional products are quickly becoming software, and how that allows for a split between the competitive power of organizations and their money making potential. And you will learn how the availability of data sparks an endless stream of new products and services that impact both business and society. In chapter 4, I will show how three global events are driving the changes I describe in this chapter.

These three 'drivers of change' are the critical issues in developing successful data driven business models that I describe in parts 2 and 3 of this book.

Information Generations

In his book, Friedman describes how neither governments nor institutions drive change, but a 'shared ability' of users. The information generations theory describes how users have changed in the way they consume and connect data and how this change has paved the way for shared ability. It explains how younger generations use ever faster media to gain access to and harness an ever increasing amount of data. Younger generations tend to make more decisions than their predecessors, based on less in-depth knowledge per topic but about a broader range of topics. The theory is by no means a scientific approach but an illustration of what is happening in decision-making structures, how that impacts the competitiveness of organizations and how this in turn shapes the nature of the media we use. That change in media usage is one significant factor that drives data-driven strategy.

The Newspaper Generation

Judging by today's standards, people born before World War II had very limited access to data in their working life. Telex exchanges increased in popularity after the war, but the primary means of communication were the mail, the newspaper and the telephone. Business people in this era were used to discovering a lot of information about a given subject but only when strictly necessary since data gathering was a time consuming task. This was reflected in their decision-making methods. Before making an important decision, the 'Newspaper Generation' would ensure being as well informed as possible, collecting all possible information before deciding. Decision-making was an elaborate process and not to be taken lightly. Even when telephone and telex increased the speed of decision communication, paper-based information remained the fundament of knowledge and insights.

The TV Generation

In the 70s and 80s not the newspaper but the television became the medium of choice. In the early 1990s, CNN covered the news in real time, and though newspapers remained the predominant news source, they no longer covered the scoops but instead provided valuable insights and detailed explanations that television could not or would not offer. In January 1991, CNN's Bernard Shaw definitively placed television news media at the forefront of news coverage when he proclaimed that 'The skies over Baghdad have been illuminated' in his announcement that the first Gulf War had started. Simultaneously, mobile phones were becoming prevalent in business life even though 'mobile' was hardly a fitting description.

The 'TV Generation' changed its decision-making compared to the Newspaper Generation in the sense that it had less in-depth knowledge about a broader range of topics than the generation before it but was able to link pieces together far quicker and easier, allowing it to decide and communicate these decisions quickly. This effect literally caused business to 'speed up'.

The Nintendo Generation

The advent of the Internet in the second half of the 1990s would have an exponential effect on this increase in speed. In a matter of 20 years, the way that business was done had changed from one based on newspapers, mail and telex to TV screens in offices showing CNN, mobile phones and e-mail. The new kids on the block, only ten years younger than the average TV Generation, grew up processing over 3000 advertisement impulses per day and playing computer games that trained them to make almost instant decisions based on very limited and mainly visual information. This 'Nintendo Generation' replaced CNN with web-based news and RSS feeds published on their cell phones. In many ways, the Nintendo Generation and its urge to speed up the decision-making process has sparked technology to move in that same direction; RSS feeds, Twitter and Web 2.0, the trend to put applications and information online for faster access, can be seen as a reciprocal trend.

The Mobile Generation

The latest branch of information generations is dubbed 'Mobile Generation'. It is the generation that cannot remember how people went online without a mobile phone, just like many people cannot remember how we got cash from the bank without ATMs (just as a reminder: we used paper checks and made face-to-face withdrawals inside a building). But the Mobile Generation appears to break with the tradition that decision-making is based on less-but-faster information. Quite the opposite, the Mobile Generation is quickly mastering the skills to collect more information. Much more. In fact, 'Mobilers' are increasingly able to collect virtually every last bit of data necessary, wherever they are, to make a decision in real time. They may not necessarily be faster than their Nintendo predecessors, but they are able to collect more relevant data to support their decision.

The Mobile Generation is connected through networks and communities. They do not just search for data on the web. Mobilers use instant messaging, posts and tweets to create networks with the lifespan of one single decision, uniting people and technology to share and connect information about the topic at hand, only to dissolve the network when the decision has been made and to create new ones when required. Mobilers do not search for information about a specific topic but base their opinion and their decisions on bits and pieces gathered by and through their network. The old paradigm that knowledge is power is quickly being replaced by the paradigm that knowledge (read: information) is ubiquitous and power comes from the ability to connect. Yes, being connected was possible before the era of smartphones, but it is easier if you don't need to be sitting in front a desktop computer all the time. So much easier, in fact, that Mobility has been a driving factor in the rise of social media.

Value Shifts from Publishers to Platforms

In the early days of the Internet, the best-valued companies online were Internet Service Providers (ISPs), the companies that sold Internet subscriptions and thus allowed people to go online. Many ISPs were quickly valued at millions because, investors figured, they controlled who had access to what. Their value initially lay in the number of subscribers, which leveraged a certain monthly income in subscription fees. But after a few years, the number of subscribers was interpreted less as a guaranteed income in monthly payments and more as a guaranteed number of visitors to the ISP's homepage, which would be the default homepage in the user's browser. The value, therefore, was not built on subscription fees but instead derived from controlling who looked at what. In that context, the ISP homepage proved a very attractive page for advertisers.

A few more years later, the (as it turned out) overvalued subscribers did not generally remain loyal to their ISP's homepage. ISPs realized that publishing interesting content was a whole different ballgame from providing Internet access. They lost the battle for the users' attention to professional publishers, who by then had had plenty of time to practice making the most of their online presence. Publishers were now the new online value creators thanks to their insight into who was looking at what. The value lay in the number of eyeballs that could be directed at any given advertisement. The content on their pages was important, not due to its inherent value but because it was interesting enough for the user to tolerate advertisements next to it.

In the last few years, the rising importance of user-generated content has instigated another shift. 'Traditional' online media has been fighting off competition from content created by individuals or loosely organized networks of people. Even though these individuals are, by themselves, no threat to advertising revenues of online publishers, the sheer number of private publishers that find an audience and use simple-to-use advertising systems such as AdWords has severely disrupted the industry.

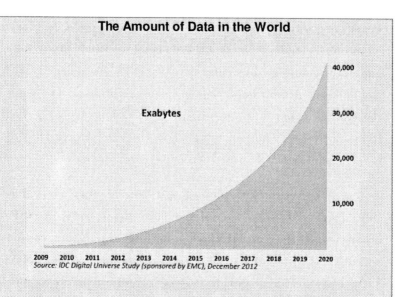

The digital universe: 50-fold growth from 2010 to 2020.

The amount of data that is available in the world is mushrooming. In large part this has to do with the format that the data is being generated in. For instance, we create many more photographs and videos on our mobile phones than we did before 2007, when the iPhone launched the smartphone era. These photographs and videos use up enormous amounts of data. But even with that factor taken into account, the amount of data that is available to people has increased (and will further increase) at near geometric rate. That is only possible because we, the people, find new behaviors to deal with this data. But there is another thing: we, the people, do not only seem to 'deal' with the rising amount. We actively seek out new applications and apps to give us more. Rather than the generations before them, who were actively trying to 'make less of more' information, the Mobile Generation is making 'more of more', sparking the growth of even more data.

Literally millions of blogs, websites and Twitterers have taken a large chunk of the market for business and entertainment publishing. Some blogs, like The Huffington Post, have become professional publications themselves. In the case of the blog Julie & Julia, it became so popular that the story of the blog's success was converted into a book and a Hollywood movie.

It will therefore come as no surprise that recently the most highly valued companies are those that control *how* people publish. The value is shifting from the ability to serve contextual advertising to marketing the knowledge of what people write and talk about. The value is shifting from the community as a place to advertise to readers to a place where companies can learn about people's preferences and behavior. Organizations like Facebook, Twitter and Wordpress have become publishing giants. Around the summer of 2011, Facebook was valued at no less US$100 billion. Not because of its advertising revenues (in fact, at the time of its IPO, Facebook was heavily under fire for its lack of mobile advertising revenues) but because it controls a mindboggling amount of data about a lot of people and operates a core process that continues to collect more data every day.

The reason why these organizations are being valued so highly is not the fact that they control what people publish. In fact, they could not stop a single user from publishing something they do not agree with, nor can they stimulate users to promote something they like. But they do have the ability to continuously know what people publish and talk about. They have created insights into people's preferences and interests. About who talks to whom and what about. About who knows who and how well. And they have gone one step further than that: they have built functionality into their websites that allows users to quickly exchange information between their website and any other site in the world and vice-versa. They not only know about what is being said on their own platform; they know what is being said throughout their 'connected environment'. The value therefore is not so much in the functionality that these companies offer but in the data they generate through that functionality. It is the same trend that is also visible in the software industry.

Data Drives Market Insurgents

In August 2011 Marc Andreessen, the creator of the world's first web browser and founder of the iconic Internet company Netscape Communications, wrote an influential essay in *The Wall Street Journal*. It was titled 'Why Software Is Eating the World'.[3] In the essay, Andreessen claims that in almost all businesses, software has become the dominant technology. The largest bookstore in the world, Amazon, is a software company. The largest music company, Apple, is a software company. The fastest growing telecom business, Skype, is a software company, and financial services have almost all transformed into software. Andreessen has a good point. In fact, his prediction that 'over the next 10 years, the battles between incumbents and software-powered insurgents will be epic' has come true almost instantaneously. But there is a nuance to his claim: software is the enabler of the insurgence. Data is quickly taking over as the driver of it.

Amazon is not the largest bookstore in the world because it runs a website but because it uses data analytics to create highly targeted recommendations. Spotify is quickly taking market share away from Apple in the music market because it uses data to create smarter radio stations. And banks are losing their software battle to Mint.com because Mint.com takes the customer's perspective to the household expenses application and linked multiple data sources to gain a complete overview of users' expenses. Data is not taking over the role that software has in the way Andreessen meant it. Software is the mechanism by which data becomes a usable product. Most competitive battles will be fought over functionality and the usability of the user interface. They are the added value that the user bases his or her preference on for a particular provider. In traditional companies, this added value was directly related to the turnover: the customer paid for the superior added value of the service. Customers like Netflix's selection of series and movies and their user interface is better than those of Hulu or HBO, so they subscribe there. As a result, Netflix makes a higher profit and wins. Yet in data-driven strategy, the customer benefits (and thus the company's competitive power) are not directly related to the turnover but to the generation of data. If Netflix starts to leverage the data it generates from people watching series, its competitive position changes. As Andreessen pointed out: 'Software is eating the world'. Traditional products are quickly becoming software, but their revenue generation capability is increasingly found in the data that this software generates.

As more and more products become software and an increasing flow of data becomes available to the world, a necessity arises to change this data into marketable products and services. After all, data by itself is not a product; it requires a service to be interpreted, analyzed or combined with other data to leverage its value. It turns out that the best people to find good uses for this data are not the people that created it. Data availability, it appears, sparks creativity in many.

Availability Sparks Creativity

Data shares many features with the famous Lego toy blocks: it comes in small blocks that can be joined to create a bigger shape. The blocks come in different shapes and colors and allow for endless combinations and variations to create almost anything. Like Lego, information sparks creativity. With lots of data we can do things we never could before. Google Maps, Twitter-based businesses, Mint.com-type analysis tools would never have come into existence if people hadn't seen the data. The data was not collected to feed the initiative; the initiative was born out of the availability of data. At this moment, thousands of start-up businesses and established companies are inventing new applications based on data they obtain from internal or external sources. This trend could not have happened at this pace if the raw material was not data. Data is easily transported, shared or copied. Data works extremely well in connected environments and in any location. And most of all, people love data. As I demonstrated before, information generations increasingly rely on data from connected sources. From individual 'publishers' in their networks. Through apps and social networks. Not in one predictable way, but in fluid, creative ways. Data Lego is the ideal source material.

In the summer of 2007, three colleagues at Stamen Design, a design and technology studio in San Francisco, launched a website that would make a significant difference to the people of Oakland by doing little more than presenting data that had been accessible to them since 2002 in a different way. They took freely accessible data about crimes in the city of Oakland, categorized the information by type of crime and plotted it on an easy to navigate map of the city. In short, they took dull and impractical statistics and turned them into visible and useable insights about crime rates and the evolution of crime in different areas of the city. They turned information that was already out there but hardly used into information that could not be ignored.

Michal Migurski, director of technology at Stamen, knew the power of maps in putting data into perspective. His company specializes in design around interactive maps. In 2007, Migurski and two colleagues decided to plot the freely available crime data, provided by the city of Oakland, onto the map of the area where he lived. They created a newsfeed that would alert them of crimes in their region and allowed them to verify this data on a map of their neighborhood. But they went even further: they categorized crimes by date and had an animation visualize the evolution of crimes in the area, day by day, week by week, month by month. The police already categorized crimes by type, so they color-coded each crime on the map. The interactive crime map served as both a demonstration project for Stamen as well as a serious attempt to serve the community by informing them about their environment. The attempt certainly paid off. Crimespotting.org quickly became a much visited website by Oakland residents.

Oakland police would traditionally respond to individual crimes the moment they were reported. The planning of their routes when on duty and their presence in the area was based on experience and practical knowledge of the developments in the city. They knew where and when to expect misconduct and positioned themselves to respond as best as they could. Their activities were focused on crime and crime prevention.

Crimespotting.org impacted police behavior in an unexpected way. As time passed, the citizens of Oakland increasingly contacted the police about events that had taken place in their neighborhood or on their commuting routes. They would use the animations on Crimespotting.org to demonstrate that their traveling routes were becoming increasingly dangerous or that a spree of burglaries was impacting their residential area. Previously, civilians had had no way to prove their hunches about crime evolution. But now the proof was there for all to see. The Oakland police rose to the occasion, and instead of dismissing this civilian 'intrusion' into their profession, they switched their focus from crime and crime prevention to those they were serving in the first place: the law-abiding residents of Oakland. In cooperation with the citizens, Oakland police now analyze crime using Crimespotting.org technology and set up action plans to fight crime where it is most effective.

The Crimespotting.org case is a very compelling one. Not only does it show how data can be used to analyze and fight crime, it shows how data sparks creativity. The Oakland police registered crimes for administrative purposes and by sharing the data with the public gained a service to actively help Oakland citizens make their neighborhood safer and bring police and citizens closer together. Inspired by the success of Crimespotting.org, Michal Migurski is now actively encouraging local governments to use his technology to visualize other data such as tree plantings, new schools, applications for liquor licenses, and any other information that matters to people who live in these neighborhoods. Thanks to the Obama administration, the data that Migurski is looking for is usually already available online.

Because of the Open Government Initiative led by Beth Noveck, by 2013 some 389,000 different datasets were available to the public. These had been downloaded more than 2 million times.[4] The applications are numerous and include websites and services from Crimespotting.org to applications that improve the National Health Service. But open data is not just limited to public services. More commercially oriented applications include the independent public initiative FlyOnTime.us, where travelers can find the flight most frequently on time between two airports or check if and how badly their flight is delayed. The site combines data from various US government sources and adds data sent in by users' cell phones about waiting lines at check-in desks. As if it were Lego.

4 - Three Drivers of Change

How three big events paved the way for new business models

The examples of change from the previous chapter are indicators of socio-economic and technological trends that are happening today. Individually, they are not causing a revolution or new business paradigm. None of them is the single driving force behind our hunger for data or the new business opportunities that this hunger brings with it. However, in combination with similar developments, they are driving three major economic events. This chapter describes these three events and how they pave the way for businesses to engage in data-driven strategy.

The first economic event and driver of change is what I call the 'connected economy'. No technology can trigger economic and social changes without people actively adopting it and applying it in their environment. Before the Mobile Generation, people's adoption of information technology was usually aimed at doing the same thing faster. But the Mobile Generation (and, in its wake, the older generations adopting its methods) is taking a different approach: it does things not faster or better but differently. It connects into networks and shares and cooperates. This is not a unique feature of this generation; people and business have been connecting increasingly over the past twenty years. But the recent social media hype, ignited by the Facebook generation, has caused a tipping point in the Connected Economy, both for individuals and for businesses. It has led to both the technology and the mindset to connect more often and for more reasons.

With the increasing connectedness and connectivity of people, so increased the connectedness of devices that has become known as the 'Internet of Things'.[5] This is the second driver of change. Being mobile and connected drove the need for constant communication and information as well as the need to connect devices to the central network in the Connected Economy, the Internet. It is the stream of data coming from these devices that sparked a good deal of the data creativity I mentioned before. In turn, the applications that sparked from that creativity drove more demand for sensor data.

The third driver of change is the fact that people have become far more mobile. They tend to travel further and more frequently, and at the same time they are less bound to specific locations. Mobile devices such as smartphones and tablets have emerged as a result of this trend and likely have enabled its rapid growth. Their existence has sparked another mobile development: location-based services. On the road we have more to publish about, more data to share and more creative and fun applications to use based on that data. The fact that people have become more mobile has led to a fully fledged infrastructure that enables us to work and live efficiently whilst on the road. And at the same time, that technology drives us to do more things in different locations.

Each of the three drivers of change causes a flywheel effect: the Connected Economy, Internet of Things, and Mobility. And each of them influences the other. In Data Driven Strategy, it is these three drivers of change that directly influence every business model focused on data—and the customers that it serves.

The Connected Economy

Today, virtually every business is in some way or another connected to suppliers, partners and customers within an integrated business model. This Connected Economy has quickly become the norm. In their influential book *The Future of Competition*, C.K. Prahalad and Venkat Ramaswamy not only recognize the importance of collaboration between various market parties, but they claim that in order to gain a competitive advantage in the future, organizations must collaborate closely with their (individual) customers.[6] The origin of this shift lies in the increasing bargaining power of buyers due to the emergence of communication between customers. The Connected Economy, in other words, is most certainly not limited to companies but applies to customers in the same way. One particular event in the 1980s, long before social media was empowering customers, one single customer and his supplier hesitantly took the first steps to what we now regard as the Connected Economy.

In 1987 Sam Walton, founder and chairman of Walmart, and Lou Pritchett, a close friend who was then VP of sales at Procter & Gamble, went on a canoeing trip. It was on this trip that both men decided it was time for the largest supplier and the largest customer in the United States to work closer together and optimize the processes for mutual benefit. Walton had realized that electronic messaging could render a good part of the complexly organized P&G sales force for Walmart unnecessary. In turn, Pritchett had realized that P&G's involvement in 'total quality management' might just be extended to improve the relationship with Walmart. The two men discussed the possibilities and realized their companies had a lot to gain from working closer together. Shortly after the canoeing trip, John Smale, chairman of P&G, called Sam Walton and invited him to visit the P&G head office to discuss the cooperation.

In his book *The Walmart Way*, Walmart's former COO Don Soderquist recalls how this trip almost didn't take place.[7] Sam Walton, the cost-conscious retailer, had discovered that the hotel they were staying at in Cincinnati cost over one hundred dollars per night, which he thought was far too expensive. When he complained about this to P&G, Walton was swiftly booked into a different hotel costing just fifty-nine dollars per night. (Later, it came out that instead of changing the hotel, P&G had picked up half the bill.) The meeting between the two giants that followed was the beginning of a textbook example of business connectivity. Within a few years after the meeting, Walmart and P&G were exchanging sales data for Pampers, allowing P&G to automatically restock over 2,000 stores with diapers without Walmart undertaking any action. From there, the cooperation quickly extended to other lines of business, paving the way for business connectivity to become a world wide standard.

The next big step in business connectivity came about a decade later and was made by e-commerce pioneers Amazon and Dell. Amazon, at that time still only selling books, surprised the world in April 1998 when it acquired the Internet Movie Database (IMDb.com), a website listing information about movies. The company had plans to launch a DVD shop later that year and realized that connecting to the world's largest repository of movie information, created by the worldwide audience itself rather than an editorial staff, would dramatically impact the already impressive system of recommendations. What better place to sell a DVD than on the page where it was discussed by its biggest fans? Dell, in turn, became famous for connecting computer component manufacturers, logistics providers and web services specialists to create one of the first fully integrated online computer retailers. Dell proved that exchanging data makes organizations more agile and competitive.

From a business perspective, the Connected Economy lies at the core of the information age. However, this book does not merely focus on the interactions between organizations and their openness with data because connectivity is rapidly expanding beyond the organizational domain. Individuals, both from within and outside of organizations, are connecting to form groups based around special interests and expertise. Much faster and certainly more unpredictable than their organizational counterparts, these connected individuals influence and inspire the exchange and use of information. Not only from the perspective of personal interests, but interestingly from the perspective of the organization as well. Individuals are quickly starting to use their 'social connectedness' to the benefit of their jobs.

People are social creatures; we connect. This basic principle predates the Internet. It has been true since the dawn of time. The Internet merely accelerated connectivity. Although e-mail and the Web have brought people together in a way that surpassed every other single invention, it by no means created an instant 'Connected Economy'. The paradigm shift did not happen overnight, nor is there a single cause that made it happen. Social applications such as Facebook or Twitter would not likely have caught on in the first ten or so years of popular Internet. But slowly and surely, because ever more people and ever more 'things' became connected to the Internet, more people connected to each other and to each other's networks. Professional networks such as LinkedIn (launched in 2003) and consumer networks such as Facebook (launched in 2004) marked the tipping point in social networking and started the trend in social media. A trend that was accelerated even more by the appearance of the smartphone in 2007, which enabled people to use social networks in any imaginable location. It was one of the key drivers for the rise of the Mobile Generation

In his book *Socialnomics*, published in 2012, Erik Qualman describes the rise and impact of social media. The book presents some striking statistics about social media usage that form an interesting indication of the impact of the Connected Economy on daily life:[8]

- 1 in 5 US couples have met online and 1 in 5 US divorces are blamed on Facebook

- One new member joins the business network site LinkedIn every second

- Various famous musical artists have more followers on social media than the population of average sized countries

- 69% of parents are 'friends' with their children on social media

- Every minute, some 24 hours of video is uploaded to YouTube

- 34% of bloggers post opinions on products and brands

- 93% of marketers employ social media for business

Although most of these statistics are now outdated and none of them proves a particular point, they offer a good sense of how the economy has changed over the last 10 years and what is meant by the popular term 'connected'.

Social media connects people through 'friendships', like-buttons, Twitter-messages and share-location services and form an important part of the Connected Economy. However, the realm of connectivity extends to a host of other developments. It includes concepts such as 'Wikinomics', which describes how the Internet allows users to, for instance, exchange experiences, leverage group-buying power and engage in customer driven product development. Connectivity is also used in initiatives such as crowdfunding, where companies and individuals attract groups of people to invest in their new developments or ideas at the earliest stages of development. It is central to the phenomenon of co-creation, as predicted and described by Prahalad and Ramaswamy on page 2 of their publication *The Future of Competition*:

"Consumers have more choices that yield less satisfaction. Top management has more strategic options that yield less value. Are we on the cusp of a new industrial system with characteristics different from those we now take for granted? [...] The answer, we believe, lies in a different

premise centered on co-creation of value. It begins with the changing role of the consumer in the industrial system."

The Connected Economy has fundamentally changed social behavior and the way business is conducted between companies and their customers. Also between companies and their employees. Even amongst colleagues. The Connected Economy changes the way people work in sales, with an increasing number of sales reps relying more on LinkedIn for their relationship management than on their CRM systems. It changes the recruitment procedures in HR departments, with more and more people being recruited through Twitter and Facebook than through traditional campaigns. And it changes the way people work in marketing, where viral and social campaigns are no longer the exception but rapidly becoming the norm.

The Connected Economy has changed the world in another interesting way. Before the millennium, new technology developments were usually aimed at and available primarily to the business user. The latest laptops were first made available to the best sales representatives, mobile phones were introduced to business executives and market data was exclusive to high paying corporate clients. But the Connected Economy has shifted the balance in favor of the consumer, a consumer who has simultaneously become a very demanding employee.

Increasingly, driven by their personal experiences and access to data, employees often harass their corporate ICT departments, claiming that their personal laptops and smartphones are newer and faster and come with far fewer limitations and security constrictions than corporate-issued hardware. In fact, many employees go to great lengths to avoid using corporate hardware or software in favor of their personal tools. They communicate with colleagues through Whatsapp groups that they setup and configure themselves. They share files on Dropbox and bypass e-mail attachments limits by sending very large presentations through WeTransfer. And in data, many employees find that personal or free subscriptions to data or data sources offer more flexible access to information than corporate subscriptions. They set up search queries in Google News and have an e-mail alert sent to them whenever their competitors or other relevant business issues are mentioned. They combine Twitter messages from colleagues, competitors and industry leads with LinkedIn Group updates to construct targeted business overviews. The Connected Economy has empowered people in their private lives and at work. But just as it enables people to get access to data, it generates an equal amount of it. New data that companies need to harness and use. Because with people working more from home, hotel lobbies, and restaurants, as well as using location-based services and social media, they might inadvertently be giving away just a bit more than they would like.

The Internet of Things: A Sensory Revolution

In 1999, Kevin Ashton, then brand manager at Procter & Gamble, was presenting his ideas about the impact of radio-frequency identification chips (RFID chips) on the P&G supply chain to a group of executives at his company. The presentation would become famous as the place where the term 'Internet of Things' was first coined. Ashton would later explain that at the time "linking RFID in P&G's supply chain to the then-red-hot topic of the Internet was more than just a good way to get executive attention".[5] However, he wasn't just looking for management attention to make himself look good. Shortly before the presentation, he had founded the Auto-ID center, the RFID research consortium at the Massachusetts Institute of Technology. RFID technology consists of small chips the size of rice grains that can be embedded in almost anything, from products to pets and even humans, and that can register and transmit virtually any type of data. He was thoroughly convinced that RFID could give P&G a competitive edge and a head start for the future. Ashton's vision of RFID was that of an enabler for what he so famously called 'The Internet of Things'. Computers, so Ashton reasoned in 1999, have always been limited to the input of human-generated data. The possibilities of computing power could be so much more useful if computers were able to sense by themselves. 'We need to empower computers with their own means of gathering information, so they can see, hear and smell the world for themselves, in all its random glory. RFID and sensor technology enable computers to observe, identify and understand the world — without the limitations of human-entered data.' In Ashton's vision computers connected via the Internet would be able to communicate amongst themselves based on their own perception of their environment. He called this 'The Internet of Things'. Fifteen years later, his vision has become a fast growing reality.

Organizations like RFID and sensors because they like to measure things. Shops collect cash register data, measure the volume of store visitors and track shoppers' movements through the store. Logistics companies track the position and movements of their vehicles, the speed at which they travel along every part of the route, the number and size of parcels they deliver to each customer and their origin. Energy companies use smart meters to collect data every second about the usage of electricity or gas in private homes and offices. The minute you switch on an appliance in your home, the energy company can detect the power profile of the appliance. The first few seconds that an appliance is switched on, it uses a specific intensity of electricity to 'load' all electrical components in the appliance with energy. This load, when plotted on a graph, would show a unique and distinguishable chart line visualizing exactly which appliance was switched on. By comparing this power profile to a database of all known appliances, the energy company can ascertain which appliances you have in your house and at what times and how often you switch them on or off. Simultaneously they collect data on every last detail in their power plants such as the amount of coal used per minute, the carbon dioxide content of this coal, the amount and temperature of cooling water they discharge in a river and the flow speed, temperature and nitrogen dioxide emissions of the smoke from their chimneys.

In an article written in 2010, scientists at HP envisioned a world with one trillion sensors.[9] In 2011, Cisco predicted some 50 billion devices would be connected to the Internet in 2020.[10] Even though it would be very difficult to measure exactly how many sensors are collecting data and loading it onto the Internet, one thing is certain: our world is swarming with sensors, some in very unexpected places. They can be found in the soil, in rivers, in the oceans, in the atmosphere, in and on animals, in bridges, buildings, cars, machines. Sensors are everywhere. Their data is increasingly placed online the very second it comes into existence. Sensors have already far outpaced humans in connecting Internet to the physical world. In a broad sense, sensors are not limited to physical measuring devices. In fact any point at which systems, hardware or software register a fact can be considered a sensor.

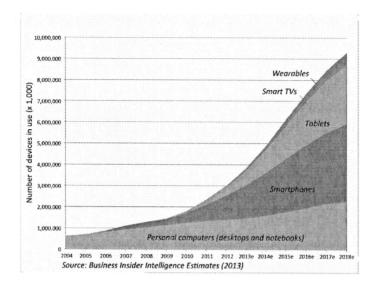

Figure 1 The number of connected devices, estimated until 2018 (Source: Business Insider, Dec. 2013)

Today, any opportunity to collect data is seized even if the collectors do not yet know what to do with all that data. This is the case for any online application that easily generates and stores information. In turn, the availability of this data has sparked the ambition to be able to collect data that does not originate online with the same ease and flexibility. It is no coincidence, then, that at the same time the data revolution began online, the market for remote sensor technology boomed. Within a few years, RFID has become the predominant standard for remotely reading data from products. RFID chips are so cheap and small that they can easily be placed into even the smallest objects. Even though the chips themselves cannot be considered sensors, the devices that read the data from the chips are. Every time they sense a chip, they generate data.

Initially, the chips and sensors were placed only in those locations where the data they generated was immediately used for a specific purpose. But the availability of data quickly encouraged creative minds to think up more uses for the same technology, expanding the use and value of the sensors.

In retail, a well-known example of RFID is the tracking and tracing of inventory and the automation of the ordering and logistics process. If all packages of individual products were to have an integrated RFID chip (instead of a printed barcode) a warehouse employee could stand anywhere inside the warehouse and scan all available products inside the warehouse with the single press of a button. His device would simply send out a radio signal to all RFID chips, which would respond to the device by transmitting their product code. The device could then determine which packages responded and, by using GPS technology, could even indicate the location of each individual package within the warehouse.

This example is everyday practice in many warehouses today. The chips placed in each package mean the possibilities for other uses are virtually endless. What if the packaging was a milk carton in a supermarket? The reader could be built into a shopping cart equipped with a small display. This display could inform the shopper, for instance about the total price of all items in the cart. If the cart could also read the RFID chip in the shopper's loyalty card issued to him by the supermarket, the cart could also alert the shopper to the fact that he might be forgetting something he regularly buys. Now link all of this data to the Internet and build an RFID sensor in the shopper's fridge at home, which could then connect the cart to the fridge to see if, for example there was any milk left. Should milk supplies be low, the shopping cart could alert the user and remind him to buy milk. The example is futuristic and maybe a bit far-fetched, but technically it is a realistic possibility and a good indication of what effect sensors have on the volume of data that is currently collected and transmitted. Measurements create data, and the use of that data generates more data. The availability of all of this data sparks creativity. So much creativity, in fact, that the Oak Ridge National Laboratory has started an initiative called 'Sensorpedia', a public website where individuals, communities, and enterprises can share, find, and use sensor data online.[11] A special programming module (API) allows software developers to immediately connect their applications to sensor data shared from other parties, the idea being that facilitating availability of sensory data will spark even more creativity. With the cost of sensors dropping dramatically and organizations around the world making sensor data publicly or commercially available through easy-to-use Internet applications and worldwide standards and formats of data, the wealth of available data is literally mindboggling.

In general, companies tend to follow one of two strategies when it comes to sensory data availability and analysis: the first is to measure what needs to be managed. The organization goes out to measure or find everything it needs to know on a given subject, collects it and analyses it to reach a conclusion or decision. Everything else is dropped. The consequence is that companies are very well informed about what they know they need to know but are likely to miss opportunities based on available data that they did not collect or measure.

The second strategy is to measure everything that needs to be managed and in addition collect data about everything that may seem relevant to analyze but has no immediate goal or proven result. The idea is to dive into the data to analyze it and come up with opportunities and solutions to previously undiscovered problems. This is the science of 'data discovery' or 'data mining'. One example of such a strategy is pattern recognition in customer data. Supermarkets, for example, generate enormous amounts of data through their cash registers, which they combine with weather data and broadcasting schedules from television networks to discover visitor and spending patterns related to major sports events, hit shows or blockbuster movies.

Mobility

With the launch of the iPhone in 2007, the world changed. The iPhone, quickly followed by a whole range of other smartphones, brought mobile broadband Internet and serious mobile applications within the reach of millions. Five years later a billion smartphones and tablets were in circulation. They impacted not simply communication or work methods. Smart mobile devices changed the way people communicated, worked and lived. They kick-started social media platform Twitter, changed Facebook and, through the concept of 'apps', opened opportunities for entirely new lifestyles. In business environments, the iPhone was the first real competition for BlackBerry, which had been the dominant phone in business since 2003. Although BlackBerry had made businesses truly mobile, the iPhone brought WiFi and GPS functionality and the concept of almost endless functionality expansion through apps. Before the iPhone, smartphones were telephones that could also be used to read and send e-mail and check a calendar if a computer was not readily at hand. The iPhone, even though the name suggested otherwise, was never a phone with additional functionality. By design it was a device for e-mailing, browsing the World Wide Web, planning schedules, using social media, navigating and oh, yeah, I almost forgot...calling people.

The iPhone quickly conquered the market with its stylish design and touch screen. A year after it launched, it was joined by competing devices from various manufacturers that used the Android operating system for smartphones, which was developed by Apple's rival Google. The availability of cheaper devices and an open source operating system caused lightning fast adoption of smartphones in all layers of society and an almost epidemic development of apps and innovative uses of mobile devices. It has placed multiple sensors in every pocket on every street corner—sensors that are directly connected to the Internet. It has put information and functionality at people's fingertips at almost any location in the world. And it placed it in the hands of an audience that was more than ready and able to discover its full potential. The concept of Mobility is much more than the availability of mobile technology. It is a reference to the way in which the Mobile Generation has adopted the technology and is changing the way people live and work.

Basically, Mobility hinges on a combination of three things: smart devices, GPS and avid users: the Mobile Generation. The smart device is a requirement because it is the single interface for people to use and manipulate information. Early versions of smartphones, such as Windows Phone models and the Nokia Communicator, failed to have the same impact on Mobility as the smartphone because they were clunky and rigid rather than smart. Smart devices use a simple and intuitive interface through the use of a touch screen and apps that perform a single task very conveniently rather than a whole suite of tasks in a complex interface.

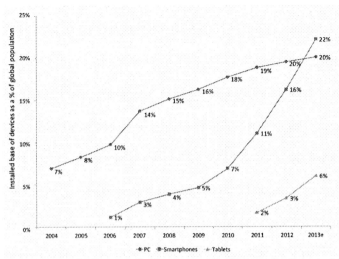

Figure 2: Global device penetration per capita (Source: Business Insider, Dec. 2013)

Apps are appealing because they can be started quickly and used instantaneously. It may seem trivial, but for people on the road it is a requirement. Speed is pivotal when taking pictures, sending a tweet or finding a phone number. As is the fact that all of this should be possible to operate with one hand. The success of smart devices was in the big details: an intuitive interface for many simple functions, with an easy way to add and remove functionality, and that is quick and takes only one hand to operate.

The second requirement for Mobility is the use of GPS. Even though many smartphones are equipped with a multitude of sensors, the one that is indispensable for Mobility is location tracking. The idea of putting a GPS receiver in a phone certainly cannot be attributed to Apple. Finnish handset manufacturer Benefon launched a GPS-enabled cell phone in 1999, but its functionality was aimed at safety in mountaineering and tracking. It wasn't until the arrival of smartphones and apps that GPS functionality could be integrated into apps developed by third parties. GPS is important because it enables apps to know where a device is and to adapt its functionality to that location. Weather apps can quickly show the weather in the current location. Shopping apps can direct a user to the nearest store, social media apps can automatically add a location to a status update or tweet and a simple 'car finder' app can help drivers pinpoint their parked car in a city where they are unfamiliar. Location-based services become even more interesting when the service connects multiple locations into a single application. The popular app 'Friends Around Me' allows users to spot which of their friends are actually in the neighborhood based on the GPS locations of their phones.

In business applications, GPS is important because it allows for the analysis of where people are when they do things. Later in this book I will demonstrate how retailers can automatically adjust the number of loyalty points they award to clients depending on their location. I will show how lease companies can offer cars at a lower rate when customers allow them to send push advertisements based on their current location. And how a sports fashion brand uses its customer's GPS-enabled phone to log their runs and exercises and to build value added services on that data.

No matter how important the device and the GPS receiver, the third and most important driving force behind the concept of Mobility are mobile users. Just like in the Connected Economy, where business environments and social behavior changed because people formed networks, business environments are changing because people become more mobile. Not in the sense that they move to more locations, but in the sense that they have quickly adapted to the possibilities that location aware online devices offer them. Mobility has changed the way in which we communicate, using Whatsapp, Twitter and Facebook. Since we have become 'smart mobile', we tend to look up anything that we do not know in a discussion, we share more photographs and experiences on social media, we pay differently for our parking, we watch TV shows on a park bench, we instantly book the nearest or the cheapest taxi. Each of these changes is small, but combined they have made our world and our economy more instantaneous. In that way, Mobility has changed consumers and their needs and demands.

For Data Driven Strategy, the concept of Mobility is of great influence. Customers now carry a device that is filled with sensors, is aware of its location in the world and has the connectivity to transmit this data in real time to the Internet. A large part of the influence of Mobility lies exactly in that last feature: the ability to transmit data online. It enables us to use the smartphone as a hub for a whole range of new devices that use the smartphone to either get data from the Internet or send data to it. In essence, it allows manufacturers to design and build sensors into almost anything that we wear or carry and to use the phone as the primary connection of those sensors to the Internet. Collectively, this is now referred to as 'wearable technology'.

Wearable technology really started in 2006 with the Nike+ program. Nike developed sensors to be attached to running shoes that allowed users to track how fast they had run and how many calories they had burned. Initially, the sensors would communicate with a runner's iPod, but after the development of the iPhone, obviously, that device quickly replaced the iPod. Not in the least because runners' data could then be transmitted to the Internet and displayed on a portal. That simple concept mushroomed in 2013. At the largest consumer electronics event in the world, the Consumer Electronics Show of January 2014 in Las Vegas, wearable technology was the biggest trend— smart watches, smart glasses such as Google Glass, fitness gadgets, including fitness bands that in addition to speed and calories also monitor heart rate and temperature. There were also a host of more serious inventions such as medical monitoring devices and even smart pills that transmit data from your intestines to your smartphone. Believe it or not, a few weeks before the show, Microsoft patented a bra that measures sweat and heart activity in order to detect emotional triggers for overeating.

Wearable technology has caught on in a big way. A number of industries are already relying heavily on the development of new applications for it such as healthcare, law enforcement and the military. These developments are quickly finding their way to industrial and consumer applications. BMW experimented with car mechanics using smart glasses to project movies as an overlay on the engine that they are looking at to display how parts from that engine need to be removed and replaced. Forklift drivers use glasses to direct them to the right place in the warehouse and pick up the right pallets, and miners wear technology to monitor their vital signs and, for instance, exposure to dangerous gasses. But that same technology is quickly moving into the consumer space.

Several programs have emerged where consumers wear technology that continuously monitors air pollution. These programs collect data through the users' mobile phones to create a real-time overview of air pollution in a particular area. Similar programs have arisen for the measurement of pollen to alert people with allergies or hay fever to the threat around them. Currently, most developments in wearable technology focus on the technology part rather than on the wearable, but some creative thinking is already underway that will change the way we wear our clothes. Fashion designers around the world are experimenting with LED lighting in fabric and connectivity to the Internet. It has resulted in anything from commercial applications, such as the Philips Lumalive promotional t-shirts that display movies and texts, to high fashion dresses that feature moving and changing color schemes and designs. So in the not-so-distant-future, we might just use Mobility and wearable technology to overcome the anxiety of what to wear at an upcoming dinner party: at the party our clothes would simply notice what people around us are wearing and adjust their color and print to be unique in the room.

Mobility is so much more than the ability for people to do what they always did but in a different location. The combination of sensor technology with GPS and an always-on Internet connection creates a new dynamic in what we do as well as in how we do it. And it sparks a new wave of data being generated and demanded in new types of applications and locations.

Enablers of Co-Creation

The three drivers of change—Connected Economy, Internet of Things and Mobility—enable consumers with powerful tools, data and the understanding to influence how products and services are used. Sensors and mobile phones with location-based services in the hands of a network of tech-savvy friends form a platform on which companies can serve new kinds of products and services that before simply could not be made.

Not only has it given companies a new kind of delivery platform for novelties created by their R&D departments, but it presents them with an empowered market that is more than willing and able to co-create innovation.

5 - Co-Creation

How companies and customers work together on new products and platforms

In *The Future of Competition*, Prahalad explains how power is shifting from a system where companies determine what customers need and are able to purchase towards networks of consumers who co-create value with producers. Prahalad wrote his book in a time when most executives would admit that the balance of power was shifting, leaving their company in an often uncomfortable, subservient role. But rather than advising a strategy for serving the empowered customer, Prahalad emphasized the need for a co-creation network in which companies and customers would work together as equal partners. He did not advise to do something different with the same infrastructure but to change the infrastructure to accommodate the new situation.

The focal point in the co-creation network is the experience that the customer has when using or consuming a given product or service. Every company should aim to optimize the experience for each individual customer, not so much by offering more elaborate features or options but by creating a platform in which the customer can interact with the organization, other customers and participants and add his or her personal influence to the experience.

In 2004, Prahalad could not have foreseen the radical changes to the environment where consumers and businesses would co-create. Keep in mind that 2004 was the year Facebook was founded, two years before Twitter's inception and three years before the introduction of the iPhone. Within five years of the release of the first edition of his book, the 'Information Age' had given way to the 'Social Age'. An age where Prahalad's customers had been given access to new technology that allowed them even greater freedom to co-create as well as the power to force co-creation upon unsuspecting organizations. The Connected Economy, which Prahalad had used as a driver for his ideas in co-creation, had been complemented by the Internet of Things and Mobility. The three drivers of change have given co-creation even more legitimacy and leverage.

Prahalad's idea of co-creation is that of a mechanism to create 'a source of unique value for consumers and companies alike'.[6] It enables a strategy in which customers become part of the solution they purchase and therefore become 'locked in' to the network with the business partners. The Lego Mindstorms example in Prahalad's book illustrates this clearly and is supported by a 2012 article in Sloan Management Review.[12] Lego Mindstorms is an electronically controlled, high-tech version of the famous Lego blocks. The electronic components include motors, sensors and a central control unit, called 'RCX', which is programmable through a PC. Lego Mindstorms is not just used by children but enjoys a fan base of adults in almost every age group. A large part of the co-creation network of Lego Mindstorms is made up of enthusiasts who create new building plans and applications for the RCX control unit and share them online. In addition, the Lego community consists of user groups in which people discuss ideas, work together on projects and meet in person. By February 2012, there were more than 150 known user groups with over 100,000 active adult fans worldwide. Their participation with Lego extends into product design, technology innovation and retail strategies. The program inspired customer initiatives such as rebrick.com, where enthusiasts can upload their own Lego designs and through a clever system can register how many parts they own to determine which new creations they can build with those parts.

The Lego example has, over the last decade, become one of the landmark examples of co-creation. However, the value that is created by the network is unique to Lego in the sense that no other company can to the same extent tap into the combined knowledge, experience and loyalty of the customer community. Even if one customer changes teams and decides to join a competitor's network, he could not take the value from the Lego network with him and the Lego network as a whole would not lose any value. Imagine being in or near such a loyal fan base: it would be quite a difficult decision to buy your children Fisher-Technik for Christmas.

Even though Lego, presented by Prahalad as a textbook example, hit a major slump and reported a huge deficit in the same year Prahalad published his book, the company has bounced back through careful use of co-creation and customer data. After a turnaround in management and a huge efficiency program, Lego was back on top in 2012 with its best results ever. Among the many reasons given by analysts for the recovery was the close relationship that Lego had with its customers and the growing adult customer base, which made up almost 10% of its turnover in 2012.

Lego obviously has an edge over many other businesses in terms of its ability to mobilize its user base to co-create. Its product line lives and breathes creativity, and its customer base is an audience sympathetic to novel ideas and bold creations. Many companies in other industries will find it difficult to co-create value in such a compelling way. Imagine being the CEO of a bank. Especially after the financial crisis, it would be rather difficult to co-create trustworthy financial products in a similar fashion to Lego and still adhere to regulatory guidelines. But it would be quite feasible to use transactional data to give customers the freedom to create their own analytics dashboards, compare spending patterns and co-create offers to save on expenses by group purchasing—for instance, on electricity or gasoline. When given access to the data, customers would be likely to find new and often unexpected ways to use the data to create value, just like the Lego fans are able to use their building blocks and ingenuity to invent new models and designs.

Today, businesses have fully embraced online technology in every aspect and are generating data at an exponential rate. Consumers have an insatiable appetite when it comes to new applications that leverage this data. But, just as Prahalad advocated, the new information generations have become more than willing and able to co-create these applications. Not just that; they are expecting to be allowed and enabled to do so. Not by being invited to customer panels or client interviews, but by actually and continuously adapting products and services together with the company. In a digital world where most products become software, that is often easier accomplished than one might expect. Prahalad calls this type of 'continuous innovation' a 'measure of the capacity to compete'. It is not about achieving major breakthroughs but about 'a wide variety of small changes, adaptations and fresh nuances'.

The three drivers of change have enabled a world where co-creation is the norm and customers increasingly form a network around the company in which they exchange data, both from the use of products and as a result of the co-creation process. The actual value of the network is not simply in the fact that the customers co-create. It is in the unique data that they create in the network. After all, without the data, the network would not exist.

6 - Data Creates Value in the Network

Why competition between Samsung and Apple is about data

In 1938 Lee Byung-chul founded a trucking company in his hometown of Daegu in what today is South Korea. He named his company Samsung. Today, some 75 years later, Samsung is the world's largest electronics manufacturer, producing everything from television sets to cameras, microprocessors to laptops. Although Samsung has been a household name in the computer industry and mobile phone business for decades, it wasn't until 2010 that Samsung became a serious contender in the smartphone and tablet market. Since then the company has dedicated itself to providing the best customer experience available. Samsung is doing this by changing its image from an electronics manufacturer to an experience facilitator. Think of it like this: where most camera manufacturers would try to outdo their competitors by thinking up more advanced features, Samsung has started simplifying its camera settings and adding easy-to-use functionality to watch and share pictures. After all, no one is interested in pictures locked inside memory cards. People want to show pictures to friends and relatives. So why should they open their laptops to download photos from the camera to a hard drive and then start up an application in order to show their photos? Samsung fitted out their cameras with WiFi so that customers can easily share photos and enable their TV sets to quickly show the photos on the television without any copying or downloading. In effect, Samsung moved the focus from camera to image, from hardware to data. The ultimate goal is to create an environment in which all devices work in unison to exchange and manipulate content created by their devices. The platform where all of this interaction can take place is the Samsung Smart Hub.

In an interview with MIT Technology Review in December 2012, Samsung's chief strategy officer, Young Sohn, declared that although Samsung is proud of each of its individual products, he believes the management of the data flowing through these devices is critical in the long term:[13]

"Samsung has always been known as a device company, a semiconductor company, and now a mobile-phone company. We make really great devices, but actually if you think of our future, it's in answering the question of how we put it all together and how we manage the data that's coming out of these devices and encourage the innovation ecosystem for our platforms. [...] I think we have probably the largest platform in the world between the devices and displays and televisions we sell. We actually provide more devices that are interacting with consumers than anyone in the world. But if you think about our experiences, it's device-centric. It's experienced by itself. It's not experienced in a connected way. So we think we can provide a lot more things than what we are doing today with an open ecosystem with our partners."

In essence, Young Sohn is saying that future competition will not revolve around the features and technologies inside Samsung's devices but around the network, or ecosystem, in which they operate.

Great technology is of indisputable importance, but it alone cannot sustain a competitive advantage. That advantage is derived from a data driven ecosystem. As predicted by Prahalad, this ecosystem is not managed by Samsung alone but co-created. Although an avid user of Apple devices himself, Young Sohn recognizes Apple as Samsung's biggest competitor in the field today. What is interesting here is that Young does not refer to their groundbreaking devices (at the time of writing, Samsung are, in fact, giving Apple a good run for their money) but to the ecosystem Apple has created. Within this ecosystem all devices work in unison and Apple has almost full control over the data being exchanged via apps and iTunes. For a moment, forget all the revenue generated by Apple devices and consider the simple fact that in the second quarter of 2012, iTunes claimed 64% of the entire digital music market. Even more impressive is that this percentage accounts for 29% of all music sold in retail in the US.

The Apple ecosystem is a force to be reckoned with for record labels, artists and consumers. But iTunes has one other trump: not only does Apple have a statistical ubiquitous knowledge of music sales in the US, it also knows exactly who bought what music and when, as all purchases are made through iTunes, where users have a named account and credit card number.

Apple knows who buys music when and where, and from this data it can determine the music preferences of their audience. Apple can analyze a new song and make a fairly accurate estimate of whether it will be a hit record or not. It is likely Apple will attempt to create the same ecosystem for movies (Apple TV), books (Apple Bookstore), home automation (HomeKit) and personal health monitoring (HealthKit). Unsurprisingly, these developments have Young Sohn worried.

Samsung will have to maintain its position as a leading manufacturer of devices. It will need to maintain and even expand its strong brand value and loyal customer base and carefully planned manufacturing processes, logistics and worldwide retail network. In addition, Samsung will need to build and exploit the ecosystem where all Samsung devices and their users operate and share data. Because without this data, Samsung will be unable to track the usage of their devices, cannot understand the habits and needs of their customers, will not be able to leverage the value that is transmitted via services and connections through their ecosystem and ultimately will be forced into the role of component assembler in other companies' ecosystems.

But this is where Michael Cusumano, distinguished professor of management and engineering systems at MIT Sloan School of Management, steps in. Studies that Cusumano conducted on a number of technology firms, including Microsoft, Cisco and Intel, show that single company networks, such as Apple's ecosystem, are ultimately dangerous.[14] In their research, Cusumano and Annabelle Gawer, assistant professor in strategy and innovation at the Imperial College in London, argue that there are two kinds of platforms that companies can create: product platforms and industry platforms. Industry platforms are like product platforms in that they use reusable components and standards. But they differ from product platforms in the sense that these components are created by different companies called 'complementors'. Industry platforms 'have relatively little value to users without these complementary products or services'. In a sense, Cusumano and Gawer state that industry platforms are preferable to product platforms. Not only because no single manufacturer is likely to be able to produce all of the necessary complementary products or services, but more importantly because industry networks tend to generate 'network effects': positive feedback loops and creativity that can grow geometrically with the growth of the network.

Obvious to Young Sohn, Apple operates a product platform that largely functions as an industry platform without allowing outside complementors into its ecosystem. It seems unlikely that Samsung will attempt to beat Apple at its own game. By employing its own product platform, Samsung could create a platform big enough to set a comfortable standard for a multitude of complementors and open enough to make participation an attractive prospect. As the instigator and controller of this industry platform, Samsung might align more compelling consumer advantages than Apple's brand value can counter. In the process, it could control and consume the network's geometrically growing network effects: positive feedback loops consisting of pure data. Data that can be turned into valuable products, used to strengthen the platform and to enable complementors to create new products and features.

Data is the both the result and the driver of this industry and the co-creation platforms as defined by Cusumano and Prahalad. Therefore, data forms the driving force behind co-creation, and as a consequence managing creation of data has become strategic. Even more so, the experience that is generated within the co-creation network is intangible except for the data that flows in and out of the network. The true value of an enterprise will lie in the network or platform it facilitates, influences and (to a certain point) controls. The only way to extract long-term value from a network is by utilizing the data that resides in it. In part two of this book, I will demonstrate how the network can be made part of an organization's business model. In part three, I will describe the importance of data creation, flow control and platform management in more detail.

PART II

THE VALUE

OF DATA

7 - Patterns

Viable business models for sustainable data monetization

Data Driven Strategy is about leveraging data from operational (often primary) processes to create sustainable value, both by leveraging co-creation and by enabling others to co-create with the collected data. There is no 'golden formula' for success, and each organization will find its own way to sustainably monetize data. For most organizations, monetizing data will be a new exercise and experience. New in the sense that it is open to many interpretations and ideas as well as to criticism and misgiving. As I mentioned early on in this book, most people in your organization will probably recognize that data has value and that it might be worthwhile to investigate how that value can be leveraged. Often, this is where monetizing data initiatives fall into the classic innovation trap: most organizations are designed to be stable and consistent production platforms. Data Driven Strategy often results in the development of new and innovative products, serving different markets and customer groups than the current business. That type of innovation usually translates into organizational change that is not very helpful in achieving short-term, bottom-line growth. So when data projects are put forward through the usual business channels, they likely require market feasibility studies, business cases and clear planning. As a result they often are put aside as high risk, low profit. Data-related projects therefore should be regarded as projects of strategic importance since they leverage the inevitable shift towards a data-driven economy and serve long-term goals.

The first task for anyone starting to monetize data is to make the concept understandable to colleagues. To get people to talk about it without different interpretations and with the same vision on future products, customers and revenue streams. The best way to do that is to draw the concept in an easy to understand, simple model that describes how the data could be productized, to whom it could be sold and how that generates revenue. And of course what would be required to do so and at what cost. Fortunately, in 2010 Austrian scientist and entrepreneur Alexander Osterwalder and a team of 470 co-creators published a very attractive and popular model for describing business models: the Business Model Canvas.[15] The Business Model Canvas offers you an excellent model to further develop your ideas about the business model for monetizing data. But most of all, it offers you a graphically attractive way to present and discuss your ideas with colleagues and senior management.

Even though each approach to monetizing data is unique, many organizations will establish similar ideas and designs and aim for similar goals. In his book *Business Model Generation*, Alexander Osterwalder (see 'The Business Model Canvas') faces the same situation in describing business models with similar characteristics or behaviors. He turned to the architectural concept of 'patterns' to describe these business model archetypes. The result was a number of business models such as The Long Tail model, based on Chris Anderson's concept of offering a large assortment of products and selling relatively few items of each.[16] Or the business model of 'Multi Sided Platforms' such as Apple, selling both hardware and the platform for music, books and movies. Or the business model based on offering items for free.

The concept of patterns applies in much the same way to data monetization. There is not one particular business model that best fits Data Driven Strategy, nor a limited set. But there are patterns that can help you understand the dynamics of Data Driven Strategy and inspire you to form your own strategies.

Each of the following chapters will offer patterns for value creation from data:

- by selling data,
- by innovating products through data,
- by swapping commodity offerings into value-added services,
- by creating interaction in the value chain, or
- by creating a network of value based on data exchange.

These patterns do not constitute the ultimate list of business models for Data Driven Strategy. New patterns will likely emerge and evolve over time, and the current patterns may be refined or adjusted. But for now they offer a clear overview of the dynamics of Data Driven Strategy on business models and an easy way to understand the communication possibilities and opportunities amongst groups. And hopefully a source of inspiration.

The Business Model Canvas

In 2010, Alexander Osterwalder and no less than 470 co-creators published the Business Model Canvas. The canvas is a strategic template for developing new or documenting existing business models. The canvas is a visually attractive way to describe an organization's value proposition, market strategy, infrastructure, customers, and finances.

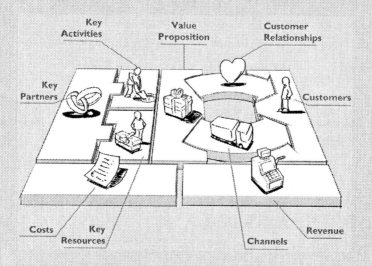

Created by jamvisualthinking.com

Since its inception in 2010, the canvas has become a standard method to describe the different interacting parts in a business model including (in the center) the value proposition, the customer segments that are served by this value (on the right) and the channels and customer interactions that are used to deliver this value to the customers. At the bottom right, the canvas displays how revenue is created from these customer interactions. The left part of the canvas describes the activities an organization needs to undertake to create and supply the value, which assets are required and which partnerships. At the left bottom the costs are displayed that are required to produce and market the offerings.

8 - Pattern 1: Basic Data Sales

How repackaging waste contributes to the bottom line

One of the simplest ways to monetize data is by simply selling it. The predisposition from which this monetization arises is that the company owns data that third parties are willing to pay for. The business model is simple: dollars for data. Although in some cases, data will need to be analyzed, repackaged and relabeled before it can be sold as product. Years ago, when I first proposed to an organization that it could resell its data, its senior management thought the idea to be preposterous. A company simply couldn't go about selling its data. I told them the following story.

Some time in the 1990s, a Norwegian company called Hydro Agri was leading the global market for so-called 'compounded' fertilizers for agricultural use, with an estimated market share of around 20%. The applications for their fertilizers ranged from increasing crops yield in traditional agricultural crops worldwide to making Middle Eastern deserts fertile enough to grow food and forage crops. However, the production of compound fertilizer creates a waste material: the chemical calcium nitrate. Calcium nitrate is not a dangerous chemical; on the contrary, it is actually a plant nutrient. But Hydro Agri did not consider it to be a viable product to market since it is naturally present in most soil types and no demand existed for it in the current agricultural markets. So Hydro's marketers tried finding applications for calcium nitrate beyond agriculture. They found one in the fact that calcium nitrate is rather effective in countering the 'rotten egg' smell caused by sulphureted hydrogen in sewers.

The waste product was offered to large European cities at a premium price to help them get rid of the nasty smell in their sewers. The solution was so elegantly simple that before long, Hydro Agri was shipping truckload after truckload of high-grade 'air freshener' to major cities across Europe. What had once been a major waste problem for Hydro Agri has now become a multi-million dollar enterprise, turning waste into a profitable business. Hydro Agri, today operating under the name 'Yara', produces and sells over 1 million tons of calcium nitrate annually.

From the day I first heard this story, it has stuck in my mind. It made me realize that for many companies data is seen as no more than a waste product. The original purpose of data includes production control, quality checks or management reporting, and after serving its purpose, it is stored in databases and neglected. Nobody seems to question the sometimes immense cost of maintaining and managing data storage and backup. But fortunately, an increasing number of managers realize that the data stored in these systems represents significant value—that it is a waste product waiting for a new purpose.

Basic Data Sales in the Business Model Canvas

The simplest pattern for monetizing data is called Basic Data Sales, or the 'repackaging of waste'. In Basic Data Sales, organizations pick up the data that is generated by their core process and sell it to third parties. Data is usually not modified although it may be anonymized or analyzed and so turned into a sellable product. It is the very first step towards a Data Driven Strategy.

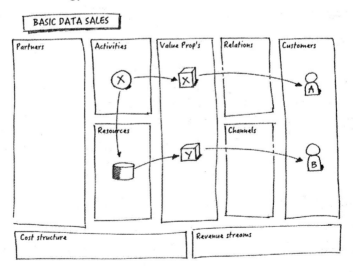

Figure 3: Basic Data Sales canvas

The canvas above depicts a bank selling data from consumers' financial transactions to retailers who are interested to learn how customers spend with them and with their competitors. In the example canvas, the company's key value proposition is the product checking account (X). This product is delivered to customer group *consumers* (A). During the production process *cash transaction* (key activity X), data is generated, which is stored in a database as a key resource. Whenever consumers use their checking account, more data is generated, which is then also stored in the database.

Although the bank's core competence is delivering *checking accounts* to *consumers*, this bank sees market value in selling the analyzed data from its database to another customer group, 'retailers' (B). The retailers are offered a data product that is effectively a benchmark (value proposition Y). For instance, household electronics retailer RadioShack would purchase an overview of the consumer spending at their stores versus the average spending of the same consumer groups at competing retail brands.

Using the Business Model Canvas to explore the potential of Data Driven Strategy offers the opportunity and advantage to explore the impact of this strategy on all essential aspects of the organization. In the example above, the obvious impact is the requirement of a new key activity, data analytics, which is required to sell data. However, since this pattern (selling data) is not a strategy in itself, the organization could in fact consider using partners to perform this new data analytics task.

Barclays Bank:
Selling Market Shares from Transaction Data

One of the most cutthroat competitive markets is retail. Especially in times of crisis, retail companies need every thin layer of margin they can get to stay on top of their business. British Barclays Bank rose to the occasion, and in October 2013 they started selling anonymized retail benchmarks to UK retail chains.[17] Put simply, Barclays counts how much money a customer spends at the selected retailer and then compares it to that same customer's spending at the retailer's competitors. The consumer data is then anonymized and transformed in such a way that it cannot be traced back to individuals and sold to the retailer. Barclays Bank is not alone. In December 2013, JP Morgan Chase placed a job advertisement for a senior product manager for intelligent solutions. In itself this is not a very moving job title, but the description of the job indicated quite the opposite: "The Senior Product Manager is inspired by the Data Economy and the opportunity to create information-based products that reinvent business, change lives, and create new commercial value for the firm".[18]

Traditionally, banks have been very good at analyzing transactional data from their customer base, both in consumer and corporate banking. In many countries, for instance, banks have long held a reputation as the most important industry analysts, offering economic insights and market reports for specific markets and regions. Their analysis combines trend analyses of transactional data (what are people spending on products from which types of industries) with additional economic research.

With the quick rise of Business Intelligence and especially with the attention for Big Data, banks across the world started looking into the potential of data as a revenue-generating asset. Driven by the increased technological capabilities and increasing market demand, innovative data products were developed and marketed. Although the typical products specifications might differ between individual banks, their mechanisms are identical: banks analyze the spending patterns of particular customer segments with a given company, for instance a retail brand, and then sell these insights to this company. Often, the data includes a benchmark between the selected retailer's score and the average score for a predetermined group of competitors. In this way, fashion retailers such as Hennes & Mauritz (over 3,000 stores in 58 countries) or toy retailers such as Toys 'R' Us (over 1,500 stores in 35 countries) can obtain spending patterns from various customer segments across countries.

These patterns can include information on its 'share of wallet' in each segment and that of its competitors, KPIs such as *recency of purchase, frequency of purchase* and *monetary value* of each transaction, etc. Rather than boasting about their new capabilities, banks prefer to keep these new products out of the public eye because they are based on the analysis of customer's transactions. Even when the products are perfectly legal and anonymized, banks are certain to receive a barrage of criticism if the existence of such practices were to draw public attention. However, as I will show in chapter 8, analysis and monetization of banking data is likely to go much further than the example above. The only question is who will be using the data.

Practical Issues with Basic Data Sales

The idea of selling transactional data to third parties is relatively easy, but is never as simple as it looks. Companies trying to merchandise their data run into several problems. Each of these problems may seem trivial and easy to solve, but combined they are the reason why a structured and continuous process for data management is required before any data can be sold with a minimum of product quality assurance. Although the specific practical issues will differ per organization, most of the problems filter down to a few basic problem areas.

Data Quality

One of the first and most obvious problems novice data providers run into is data quality. The data they are selling comes from operational systems that are most often not dependent on the exact accuracy of the data they process. When a regional insurance broker analyzed its data in preparation for selling it, it found the largest insurance claim in the last 12 months to have been well over 12 million euros. Everyone in the company knew that this was absolutely impossible. After investigating the data more closely, the analysts found that in fact one of their new employees had mistakenly entered a date in the 'amount' field on the claim intake application. This resulted in an amount of 12042011. When the system returned an error message, the employee simply closed the initial claim and started over, but the faulty claim data remained in the system. Without the new data service, no one would have noticed or cared about this mistake, but now that the data was for sale there was a much bigger emphasis on the correct entry and maintenance of data.

Data Driven Strategy creates a pressing need for high-quality data, which is not easily visible for people working with that data from an entirely different perspective. Luckily data quality management is a profession that has been in existence for several decades, and good solutions exist for both technical and cultural issues. That area is, however, beyond the scope of this book. But besides data quality, Data Driven Strategy may introduce a new issue that requires careful attention: continuity.

Data Continuity

The vast majority of data sales will take place as a subscription service, with customers regularly receiving new, up-to-date data sets. That requires continuity in the data supply. Even though most processes in an organization seem continuous, they are interrupted more often than one would expect. One example is a factory where a series of machines produces a flow of plastic goods. The factory management plans to sell analytical data from their machines about molding temperatures, material density and flow resistance back to the raw materials provider.

The idea was sound, but when put into practice, every so often data would be missing from the data sets without a clear explanation. Research into the matter showed that machines would be taken offline for cleaning and error correction in a fairly random order. To keep production up to speed, back-up machines would be used whenever a machine came offline. But the backup machines were either not connected to the IT network, had damaged sensors that were never repaired because they were not deemed critical for the machines operation or had no sensor altogether. The machine operators were not informed about the importance to check data connections, and data was lost on every switch.

Data continuity is the process that safeguards the consistent flow of data to the systems from where the data is transformed into a product. Just as in any other production process, continuity in raw material flow is a minimum requirement for success and demands process and management.

Interference with Other Processes

Often, even to the surprise of most managers, there is an additional problem in maintaining continuity: core processes in many organizations are not as steady and continuous as one might expect. Issues like variations in production, marketing campaigns, seasonality and changes in IT systems constantly affect the data being generated even though the core process may remain identical throughout. This was the case when the marketing department of a production company decided to change the classification criteria for customer groups. It changed the settings in several data entry fields in their marketing management system and requested an IT change to add another field to its CRM system. Without knowing it, the changed settings affected the analytics of the data that was sold to the reseller network. By changing the classification criteria, the data that was registered and sold no longer matched the needs of the resellers, and the data product lost value. The only solution was to keep two sets of classification criteria: one for the marketing department and one for the commercial data product.

9 - Pattern 2: Product Innovation

How small startups are competing head-on with banks by leveraging data

Many companies would, even if they could find a market, be hesitant to simply sell their data to third parties. Their reasoning is that either they feel that selling their data may compromise their competitive position or that they can add more value by using it to create additional products and services. This is exactly the predisposition from which this pattern for monetization arises. The business model hinges around the value that the company can add to the data by creating an innovative new product.

In the summer of 2012, I found myself in a meeting room inside an international bank's head office in Amsterdam. I was meeting one of the bank's information managers, and we were discussing the strategic issue of customer intimacy. In the wake of the financial crisis, and with consumer trust at an all-time low, the bank's consumer division had launched a new strategy placing the customer first. Management had banned 'customer lock-in' mechanisms and had instead chosen a strategy of customer lifetime value, an approach based on the pretext that happy customers will earn the bank more money over a longer period of time. This development represented a significant break from the way banks had become accustomed to doing business. And one that posed some remarkable challenges. Customer intimacy requires some serious knowledge about the customer—about his personal situation, about his likes and dislikes, about his habits and needs for financial services. As it turned out, the bank had very limited information to work with, and whatever information it had about customers was mostly aimed at risk analysis, viewing the customer as a potential threat rather than an opportunity. Unless the bank could somehow leverage the ultimate source of customer behavior data: their customer's financial transaction data.

The story of this particular bank is representative for all major banks in Western economies. It is the reason why most banks turn to Big Data technology to collect and analyze as much data about their customers as possible. The idea is to create a perfect customer profile to allow the bank to offer the best advice and financial solutions to the customers' needs. All banks are placing the customer first with the aim to better serve them with their existing products, services and advice. To discover the customer's exact financial matters, budgets and dreams, banks are launching online tools such as the savings monitor, financial planning tools and online household expenses applications. These online tools use transaction data to provide customers with status updates on how long it will take them to be able to purchase their dream car, how to balance their savings, stock options and expenses and how to budget their daily lives. While helping customers to manage their finances, they provide the bank with insights into the customers' budgets and targets for large expenses, such as a new television or a car, and savings for a holiday or a wedding. Such targets specifically tell a bank about what really goes on in the lives of their customers. These applications are excellent examples of data driven product innovation: banks use their existing data to create a new service that adds value to the original products. In most cases the banks offer the new services for free. After all, they reason, the new service generates new data that is of value to the bank. A valid thought perhaps, but as I will show one that leaves banks open to competition from unexpected players.

Product Innovation in the Business Model Canvas

In the Product Innovation pattern, data generated from sales and usage of one product (or service) is used to create a second product or an addition to the original, which leads to an innovative value proposition. 'Innovative' can refer to a simple added feature or to a novel type of solution. However, the latter usually results in the most sustainable type of value propositions since they tend to become standalone products that are less dependent on the original product.

Again, a bank is used as the leading example. But this time, the bank is not merely selling data. It uses this data to improve existing products and to create entirely new offerings. It offers a 'checking account' (X) as a value proposition through key activity 'cash transaction' (X) and sells the product to customer group 'consumer' (A).

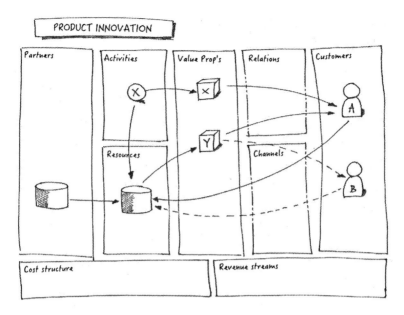

Figure 4: Product Innovation canvas

When providing the 'checking account' service, the bank generates data that is stored in a database (key resource). This data is used to create a new product, the 'household expenses dashboard' (Y), which is sold to 'consumers' (A) and a new customer group 'non-banking customers' (B) who do not have a checking account with the bank but who do use the dashboard with data from their own bank. These customers can upload their transaction data from other banks. The (transaction) data that is generated by the usage of the 'dashboard' is added to the database and is used to further improve 'online banking' and 'the dashboard' by improving comparisons of consumer's spending patterns, for instance. This analysis forms the basis of recommendations such as an alert to a consumer that his household spends far more on electricity than the average comparable household. In addition, adding data from external sources, such as current average electricity prices, may further enhance 'the dashboard'.

Competing on Data

One by one banks are discovering that the value of their data is already being used by other players to become 'intimate' with the customer. Multiple household expenses applications are already available online, most of them offered by banks. Most customers nowadays have accounts at multiple banks, yet banks do not actually allow consumers to add data from other banks, as suggested in the example for *'non-banking customers'* (B). But for customers, using a household expenses application with data from only one bank is like looking at the Mona Lisa with sunglasses on. So banks find themselves competing with applications that use transaction data from online banking applications from not just one but multiple banks, manually uploaded by the customers themselves. Commercial applications provide analytics and spending overviews in easy to use online dashboards and mobile apps. American Mint.com, acquired as a startup by Intuit in 2009, already boasted over 10 million users by the end of 2013.[19] Its competitors Adaptu and HelloWallet show rapid expansion and are being financed heavily by venture capital firms. Even in the small Dutch market, local competitor Afas already services over half a million people. Similar initiatives in France and Germany are quickly increasing their number of subscribers, gaining market share over the potential intimacy of banks.

Using the knowledge of spending patterns from hundreds of thousands of users, the vendors of household expenses tools are able to provide financial advice and sell products based on actual customer behavior. Mint.com, for instance, provides personalized offers from companies such as electricity and telecoms vendors that allow you to save money when the current expenses on such products indicate you are spending more than average users do on these categories. Not only are these services offer easy access to financial advice, they actively help customers to save money by balancing and guarding budgets and suggesting cheaper suppliers.

Technology startups from all over the world use people's financial transaction data to contest the market space banks have always claimed to be theirs: financial insights and advice. With banks' reputations shattered after the financial crisis and consumers used to being in control of their own data, the market is ripe for disruption and innovation. High-profile, high-finance institutions have come in direct competition with technology startups that center on customer intimacy and that can leverage technology to make complex products simple to understand and operate for everyone. If they succeed in taking the market for (independent) financial advice away from banks, they may just reduce the role of retail banks to that of 'transaction machines' and cause a serious paradigm shift in the traditional banking trade.

Using Data to Restore Credibility to Banking

Data driven banking competitors are emerging that are taking the household expenses application yet another step further and that venture even closer into the domain previously reserved for licensed banks. In early 2013 Movenbank.com launched an innovative mobile payment platform, receiving worldwide praise from financial and technology companies alike. Moven (the company rebranded and dropped the 'bank' from its name) and similar initiatives, such as Simple.com in the US and

Holvi.com in Europe, combine checking accounts, analytics and budgeting in mobile apps. These mobile payment platforms actually provide financial products such as a checking accounts and loans, usually based on a credit card or a third party bank account. They provide users with easy mobile payment functionality, budgeting and analytics such as online transaction overviews and smart notifications analytics.

Moven in particular adds an interesting dimension called CREDscore. CREDscore is a credibility score, which, according to the company, is significantly different from a credit rating. It is a transparent assessment of your credibility and measures in real time your financial fitness. Users are rewarded for spending, saving and living smarter to improve their financial credibility. The CREDscore is built on a wide range of data. It includes social media influence such as the number of likes a person receives on Facebook or the number of recommendations on LinkedIn. In addition, it uses answers to finance-related questions posed to the user at certain points in time. In other words, Moven deploys a wide variety of data sources to shape its engagement model.

The credibility score is an ingenious instrument that helps Moven to manage risks whilst improving customer service. It is a radically different approach from risk mitigation by traditional banks, which deny roughly 50% of all credit applications based on people's previous behavior. Moven assesses not just risk but future potential by analyzing people's financial knowledge, spending patterns, social reputation and other data. Brett King, founder of Moven, explained the idea in a 2012 article in *Wired* magazine: 'People are currently underusing their networks and reputation. [...] I want to help people to understand and build their influence and reputation, and think of it as capital they can put to good use.'[20] His views are shared by many successful business leaders, such as Ajaz Ahmed, the founder of digital innovation agency AKQA. Ahmed stated that 'in an age where transparency is the norm, what matters perhaps more than your wealth is your reputation.'[21] His opinion is shared by Steven R. Covey, author of the influential book *The Speed of Trust*, who said: 'A person's reputation is a direct reflection of their credibility, and it precedes them in any interactions or negotiations they might have.'[22]

Moven is not the only new bank to leverage social media to innovate and improve its services. Lenddo.com uses online reputation management to provide loans to the rising middle class in upcoming economies in the Philippines and Columbia. In Germany Fidor.de targets 'digital natives' by adding social functionality to otherwise reasonably traditional banking products. But Moven seems to be going just this one step further: it doesn't only appeal to tech-savvy users and collect data that is readily available from customers' public profiles. It stimulates customers to add more data about their financial behavior, their social reputation and their financial plans and targets to create a 'fluid' profile providing a wider context than just finance.

Moven uses a traditional and well-known product, the checking account and credit card from the 'old school banking' (product X), and uses the data generated by those products, the transaction data to create two new offerings: an analytical dashboard through which users can monitor and optimize their spending (product Y) and the CREDscore, an innovative product that helps to refine the original banking products and stimulates clients to use the banking products, the financial dashboard and the social media powering their CREDscore more intensely. If the CREDscore is product Z, the usage of that product drives the generation of data from the banking products (X) through smarter spending and from the dashboard through a more extensive user interaction.

CREDscore is an intricate system that clearly transcends the level of clever marketing. First of all, the score is not a classification or 'grade'. It is not a score between 0 and 10 but an ever-increasing number. It indicates how well you did in the past, but by measuring the speed at which the score drops or rises, Moven can also determine a customer's future credibility. Furthermore, users can score the most points by referring others who then prove to be credible users themselves.

Brett King explains openly that this is both a commercially inspired 'member-get-member' system and a powerful valuation within the CREDscore system. 'You can't get a high CREDscore just by gaming social networks, you actually have to be using the account everyday and saving money, thus, it's not really possible to game the system via your social media presence to get access to credit, for example. Secondly, the most impact your social network presence can have is through referral. For that to work you need to recommend Moven to your friends and they have to open an account and deposit money.'[23]

What sets Moven apart from other data innovations in banking is the fact that it does not just analyze data to give advice. It actually stimulates users to create more data. It does not just analyze past financial behavior; it stimulates users to make more transactions through their Moven account so that their CREDscore will improve. It triggers them to link to other people via social media, to sign them up for a Moven account where they generate more financial data and to discuss Moven in public and private social media messages. It does this not by some guerilla marketing tactic but because generating more data in fact strengthens the Moven product offering and the value it delivers to customers. With every bit of data that enters the system, Moven is able to make better predictions about customer behavior and to adjust its interest rates and advice accordingly. It is a system of continuous improvement. Ultimately, Moven is about creating so much knowledge and understanding about customers that the bank knows when and how it can trust them with their money.

In a somewhat ironic sense, King is using Moven to take banking back to its original role: that of an independent player vouching for the trustworthiness of its clients. After all, back in the day if you were accepted as a customer to certain banks, this meant the bank's research had shown you to be a reliable customer. Moven today aggregates people's online reputation and matches it with their financial behavior. Moven's strategy might very well be to become an independent trusted third party, providing services to any organization that requires acknowledgement of someone's credibility. Just like Google transformed from being a search engine to an advertising platform, leaving room for additional services such as e-mail and video websites, Moven may be looking at additional services to prove their consumer's trustworthiness.

Business Model 'Flip'

The household expenses applications I mentioned before—Mint.com, Adaptu and HelloWallet—have taken on banks from a data perspective. But they too are now being threatened by companies such as Moven, which are trying to gain an edge by not just controlling the data but by influencing the processes that generate it. Moven again takes the data centric approach; it does not want to be a bank because it wants to control the generation of transaction data. It wants to be a bank because it wants to allow its CREDscore data to influence conditions of the banking products. That will make users generate more specific data. One might argue that Moven is not a bank that offers a financial dashboard and a CREDscore: it is a company that offers a CREDscore and adds a dashboard and banking products to create and maintain the best possible CREDscore product.

The product innovation pattern can lead to a shift in focus, or a 'flip', when data-related turnover outpaces the turnover from the original data generating processes. It can lead to a situation where it becomes increasingly unclear whether the data that stems from original process is a waste product turned to opportunity or the primary value that is being created in that process. In traditional organizations, this may lead to confusion and in some cases even organizational discrepancies. But as the next pattern will show, for some companies flipping the business model is not incidental; it can be key to survival.

10 - Pattern 3:
The Commodity Swap

How electricity companies are
gearing up to sell refrigerators

Commodity providers are experiencing difficult times. Products like electricity, gas, water and even telephone are low interest, indistinguishable products that are mainly selected by customers based on price and brand. Online price comparison websites are not helping the companies to bring a unique value proposition to the market. So the predisposition for monetizing data is the fact that the organization sells a commodity and that data can help to build a uniquely valuable product or service.

In the last months of 2010, two Dutch senior executives, Ad Scheepbouwer and Erwin van Laethem, were chauffeured from a meeting they had both attended. Scheepbouwer was chairman and CEO of the leading Dutch telecom provider KPN and Van Laethem was COO of RWE Essent, the leading Dutch power company. Scheepbouwer has since retired and Van Laethem has continued to become the CEO of RWE Essent. Although both men were working in different industries, they had a lot in common in their work. Both companies were former government-owned utilities, both were leaders in their field, both operated in highly competitive markets and both encountered disruptive technologies that severely impacted their markets and business models. In the back seat of the car, the two captains of industry discussed their challenges and market views. The conversation, which started in good spirits, took somewhat of a strange turn when Scheepbouwer mentioned that he wanted to turn KPN into a 'smart' company. He presented Van Laethem with his vision of how telecommunications would become the vital infrastructure in making households smarter. KPN, serving millions of homes with broadband Internet connections and WiFi routers, would form the central hub for a variety of automated services in homes.

Beyond the familiar 'triple play' services (Internet access, telephone and television), KPN had plans to offer advanced home-automation products such as security applications or home care support. Scheepbouwer explained how his company would focus on service rather than infrastructure and on data rather than products. He likely added vivid examples of how all of these services would integrate; how lights would automatically dim when a 'video-on-demand' movie starts or how health monitors would automatically dial rescue services and provide them with real-time information when sensors detect unusual movements such as a fall in the house of an elderly couple. The specific ideas Scheepbouwer shared at the time are not known, but he concluded his vision of the smart home by stating that KPN could take data from a smart device, such as a thermostat or power consumption meter, and calculate how much energy a particular household would use. By benchmarking that data to other households, he would be able to tell if people where heavy users or not.

Van Laethem was taken aback and potentially threatened, certainly when Scheepbouwer implied that if he knew how much energy people were using and asked them how much they paid for it, he might as well sell them a cheaper deal. Energy, after all, was a commodity, and with delivery of the goods over a static power line, buying and selling energy was a purely administrative exercise.

Van Laethem does not go into much detail about the exact formulation of Scheepbouwer's implications, nor about his precise response. Obviously, what Scheepbouwer had described was not news to him. Van Laethem was looking at the exact same developments for his own company. Essent too had already been experimenting with home security and similar services and the option to rebrand and resell all sorts of home automation devices. After all, where KPN had a copper infrastructure into people's homes to transport phone calls, television signals and usage data, Essent, via its partner company Enexis, had access to a similar network suitable for transporting data. Both men were very aware of the importance of transporting data over that infrastructure. Both had access to all sorts of electronic gadgets that could measure and register people's activities and preferences. And both knew that their future profits did not lie in the ownership of the infrastructure or in the ownership of the data. They would lie in the translation of that data into attractive services to customers.

The car drive that had started out with a friendly conversation between two business peers had turned the two executives into direct competitors even though their businesses seemed so far apart. For Van Laethem, what Scheepbouwer had told him was nothing new. However, it made him realize that KPN and all other telecoms and TV-cable network providers like them were ahead in one important segment: customer engagement. Essent was lagging behind, and Van Laethem needed to get serious about smart energy. Although all involved are tight lipped about what really happened next, it seems no coincidence that within a few weeks after that particular afternoon, Essent hired KPN's most experienced employee in smart energy and put him in the lead team of Essent's own smart energy program.

Commodity Swap in the Business Model Canvas

In the Commodity Swap pattern, a commodity provider uses the sale or usage of a commodity product or service as a means to generate data. It then uses this data to differentiate itself from competing commodity offerings. The data is used to create a new product or service that is inextricably connected to the commodity offering. Business models vary in how this combination is monetized. In some cases the data products are offered for free in combination with an existing commodity contract. In other cases the commodity is offered at a very competitive rate while the data products are premium priced.

This time, the example business model belongs to a utility company, selling *electricity contracts* (X) as a value proposition to *consumers* (A). Its key activities include the *supply of electrical power* (X). As part of this activity, the utility company installs digital metering devices in the homes of *consumers* to measure the amount of power used by the household.

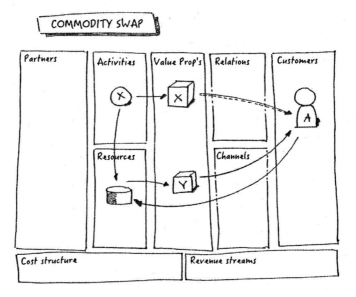

Figure 5: Commodity Swap canvas

These smart meters do not only measure the amount of electricity used, but also register additional data such as the time of use, the fluctuations on the power grid and even which actual devices are using the power. This data is sent back to the utility company, where it is stored in a database. It is then used to provide services (Y) to the *consumers*, for instance by offering variable rates during the day to stimulate power usage at off-peak times or by displaying personalized advice on a smart thermostat or a web portal. The utility company saves money by reducing peak-production capacity and generates additional turnover by charging a small subscription fee for the service including the thermostat and web portal.

Smart Meters Enable the Commodity Swap

On April 13th, 2013, Walmart issued a press release in which President and CEO Mike Duke announced that the company is aiming for a 100 percent renewable energy supply by the end of 2020.[24] In fact, the press release stated two goals: the production or procurement of 7 billion kWh of renewable energy and a reduction in global energy usage by 20% compared to 2010. The plans were announced under the flag of Walmart's sustainability program, but it wasn't the 'shift to green' that sent a shockwave through the power producing world. Walmart's announcement included plans to install solar power on at least 1,000 rooftops and facilities by 2020. At the time of the press release, Walmart had just over 200 similar installations in operation or under development.

Throughout the world, Walmart is recognized as a leader in business operations with enough scale to make a mark and set a trend. If Walmart sets this trend and a significant part of the global industry follows by cutting down on its power usage in combination with the increase of in-house production, the commoditized market will certainly take a serious beating. Bear in mind, the timeframe in which Walmart aims to realize its goals is approximately 6 years. In the world of power generation, this is considered a blink of an eye. With overcapacity looming and much of that production capacity locked in fossil fuel (i.e., 'non-renewable') facilities, the challenges are quite substantial.

In Europe and the US alike, power companies have been trying to de-commoditize their products for years by more strongly utilizing marketing and branding and offering different types of subscription plans and 'green energy' products. But the simple fact of the matter is that electricity is the ultimate commodity; it cannot be heard, seen or smelled. It is either 'on' or 'off' and never differs in quality. But it has one feature that makes it ideal for Data Driven Strategy: power networks have the ability to carry data. This fact transforms electricity from a passive bulk product to a data-carrying infrastructure for millions of homes. That is just what power companies need to add value to their portfolio and create new, distinguishable and marketable service applications. The device at the heart of this data transport is called the 'smart meter'.

Smart meters are small devices that measure the flow of electricity in a particular section of an energy grid—for instance, a house or an office building. For the record, it must be stated that smart meters are also available for water and natural gas networks, but for the purpose of this book I will focus on electricity measurement only. Smart meters measure both incoming electricity and outgoing flows over a particular time. They differ from traditional meters in the sense that they allow two-way communications and that they can detect signals, such as surge voltages on the power line. and not just the flow.

The obvious advantages of smart meters lie in the meters' capability to exactly monitor how much electricity was used and when. First and foremost, this allows for exact billing of the customer and does away with estimated periodical payments and annual corrective bills. In addition, most governments are keen to have smart meters installed as they can provide users with an exact overview of their electricity consumption and motivate them to save on power usage. Australian academics McKerracher and Torriti found that providing homeowners with real-time feedback on their electricity consumption reduces their energy consumption by approximately 3–5%.[25] In other words, the data from smart meters, when presented back to the consumer, is instrumental in lowering the carbon footprint of the nations of the world.

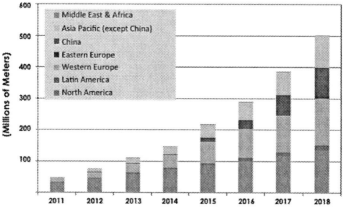

Figure 6: Installed smart meters by region (estimated)
(Source: Pike Research 2011)

From the perspective of the utility company, the benefit of smart meters lies in their capability to generate data through which value can be added to the commodity product. So much value, in fact, that in a few years' time the provisioning of electricity itself may well be regarded as the necessary mechanism to generate data rather than the activity to which features are added. Electricity companies will no longer be regarded as the provider of the necessary commodity but as the supplier of network services and data driven products.

The range of services provided by the data stream of smart meters is impressively diverse. Companies around the world are experimenting and implementing variable rates, pre-programming equipment to be activated by the power company at the best possible time, remote controlled energy savings systems, etc. But by far the most striking feature of smart meters is called 'electric fingerprinting'. Electric fingerprinting is the technology of identifying individual machines in an electricity network by measuring their specific electricity usage. The principle of electric fingerprinting was suggested as early as the 1980s, but it wasn't until 2005 that Mark Lucente of the CLP Research Institute and his colleagues from the University of Hong Kong described what they called 'A Taxonomy of Load Signatures for Single-Phase Electric Appliances' and turned theory into practice.[26] Electric fingerprinting means that a smart meter can detect not the just the fact that a machine in your house is being turned on; it can actually recognize that machine by type. With that ability, your smart meter is able to determine when you switch on your washing machine. Since all appliances have their own electric fingerprint, your electricity supplier could recognize that you just turned on your seven-year-old Siemens WXLS122.

Electric fingerprinting has many useful applications that can turn the business model of utilities into a Commodity Swap. The technology may drive a product line of services through which utilities may generate extra revenues. For instance, by comparing your washing machine's data against a global database of washing machines, your electricity company may detect that your machine is using more energy than average washing machines than run as often as you run yours. Based on that data, the company could calculate that purchasing a new washing machine would save you enough money to be profitable in 4 years' time. Should you accept the offer that they make you, you get a good new machine and the company gets a commission from the retailer.

Although the business model sounds farfetched to some, the actual ideas in boardroom brainstorms go much further. Some utilities are contemplating a leasing service in which consumers pay a monthly fee for the use of one or more electrical household machines such as a washing machine, dishwasher, dryer or oven. The lease includes the electricity used. Since the company can measure every last detail about how often you use each machine and for how long, it is able to provide you with the best quality machine for your needs that has the lowest energy consumption. If a machine breaks down or if the utility decides that installing a different machine is more profitable, the consumer gets the new machine. In every sense, this business model is fantastic example of a full Commodity Swap: the original commodity product is given away for free while the data generated by the provisioning of the commodity product drives the new revenue streams.

Whenever smart meters are mentioned, inevitably the issue of privacy comes up. It is true that there are potentially serious downsides and dangers to the unwarranted use of smart meter data. The debate about those dangers has not yet been completed and probably will lurk around for much longer. But in practice, in areas where smart meters are already in place, consumers seem to be valuing the benefits of the additional services. And energy companies in their place have taken notice of the consumer vigilance to privacy and data. Of all the energy companies I spoke to in preparation for this book, none of them are actually downloading smart meter data automatically. Each consumer must actively agree to allow electricity companies to use the data that is stored on the customer's personal website, and which remains in full control of the customer. At first glance that may sound strange from the perspective of the energy company. But as I will show later in this book in chapter 11, the issue here is not on-site ownership of the data but access and control over the flow of data.

11 - Pattern 4:
Value Chain Integration

How data defines common ground
between customers and suppliers

Monetizing data is not limited to selling data to a third party for hard currency. One different way to monetize data is by sharing it with partners in order to save on expenses. The savings and rewards can be impressive. To reap these benefits, however, companies will need to display trust and a willingness to settle payments through the exchange of data. The predisposition for monetizing data in this way is the recognition that the parties involved are part of the same value chain. As I will show in this chapter, that predisposition does not just include two companies in a direct vendor/customer relationship. Monetizing data through Value Chain Integration can cover any number of links to save money.

Michael Porter first introduced the concept of the 'value chain' in 1985.[27] Initially, Porter described a chain of events within an organization in which value was added to the product that was produced by that organization in each event. The 'links' in the chain included inbound logistics, operations, outbound logistics, marketing & sales, and service. Quickly after Porter first introduced his concept, the metaphor of the value chain expanded into that of a chain of events spanning across an entire industry.

Within the industry value chain, value is first added by the raw materials provider in the first step of the production process. After this, value is added in each step by various production phases up until the wholesale and retail functions delivering the finished products to the end user or consumer. The value chain became a key component in strategic thinking and analyzing the value, and more importantly the margin, that was generated in each of the steps. An organization's strategic decisions could then include forward or backward integration of activities in the value chain in order to achieve a higher overall margin of activities.

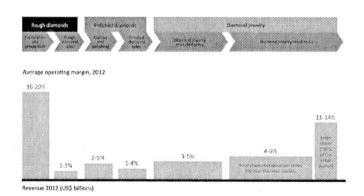

Figure 7: Example of an industry value chain (the diamond industry with revenue and average margin per segment (Source: Bain & Company, Global Diamond Report 2013)

In Data Driven Strategy, in many cases the data flow through a value chain will create significantly more value when specific data from various parts of the chain can be combined. Traditionally in corporate strategy, organizations tend to acquire operations backwards or forwards from their own position in the value chain in order to leverage the value in those segments. By and large the aim is to maximize efficiency and margin by enabling tighter integration of operations in both links of the chain.

The aim is to improve efficiency and coordination in marketing and sales, logistics, planning, etc. Much, if not most, of this integration would have to do with the exchange of data between the two entities. Not surprisingly, many post-merger integration efforts start by integrating ICT and databases. However, time and again, merger failure rates are reported between 60% and 70%. Merging two companies just isn't that simple, and in a world of increasing technology standards, integration no longer requires the actual acquisition of one party by another. Value Chain Integration allows companies to exchange data as if they were the same company.

Keep in mind that regardless of the diminishing urge to integrate business operations, the possibility of data integration in the value chain may still drive the wish to acquire companies to safeguard the flow of data to their original operations. In one such example in October 2013, Monsanto, a St. Louis based agricultural giant acquired The Climate Company, a Big Data analytics company focused on collecting and analyzing weather data for agricultural purposes.[28] The acquisition guaranteed the constant and controllable flow of important weather predictions to Monsanto farms and factories.

Value Chain Integration in the Business Model Canvas

In the pattern 'Value Chain Integration', organizations exchange data with the aim to reduce costs or optimize the performance of activities. Through the exchange of data, a supplier can more effectively respond to (or anticipate) customers' processes up to the point where it can assume full responsibility for them. The business model is not so much geared towards selling or licensing out data but towards integrating data flows to optimize operational results, reduce costs and reduce complexity.

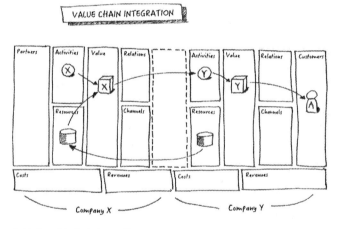

Figure 8: Value Chain Integration canvas

In the example canvas above, two companies integrate their activities in the value chain by exchanging data about supply and demand. Company Y is a food retailer with multiple stores and a number of regional distribution centers. Company X is a supplier of a range of soft drink brands, which are sold in all of the retailer's outlets. The retailer provides a real-time data feed from its point-of-sale database (key resource) to the operational systems of the supplier. The data includes how many bottles and cans of soft drinks from each of the supplier's brands were sold in each store and how often each store was resupplied with new soft drinks from the distribution center. In addition, the customer hands full responsibility to the supplier to manage the stock keeping for its products in the regional distribution centers (key activity Y). The supplier is assigned a particular space in the customer's warehouse. Using the data supplied by the customer, the supplier initiates its 'outsourced stock management' value proposition (key activity X) that effectively takes over (part of) the customer's key activity Y. The data exchange enables multiple benefits for both parties. The customer is guaranteed sufficient stock of soft drinks without allocating too much space for stocked products. This guarantees the minimum costs in warehouse space while it never runs out of stock, and in turn the supplier can control its own delivery and planning into the customer's warehouses.

Redefining Logistics Through Data

After the famous canoeing trip that Sam Walton had with Lou Pritchett of Procter & Gamble (see page 35), the two companies decided to work closely to develop a data exchange system in which Procter & Gamble would be alerted whenever stock in one of Walmart's stores was running low on a particular product. Procter & Gamble would then respond by automatically replenishing this store with the products 'just in time'. The task was far from simple. Remember that this was the age before standards such as EDI existed. This was even before Walmart or P&G could use data warehouses to support the data exchange simply because the concept of data warehousing had not been developed yet. Data exchange meant not only that computer systems had to be synchronized to 'speak the same language', it also implied that the two business had to use the same performance indicators, measurements and timeframes in order to trigger the right business actions based on the exchanged data. The team that set out to achieve all this grew to well over 250 people.

The P&G team that worked on the data systems at Walmart's office in Fayetteville were on more than one occasion known to refer to it as 'Fayette-nam'.[29] But after a year and half, P&G and Walmart were exchanging data on just-in-time delivery, and within a few years the two companies were able to exchange data on a broad spectrum of functions including transportation, finance and product development. The 250-man-strong, year-long development at times must have seemed an excessive investment, but the idea paid off in a big way: in the first year of full operational data exchange, P&G increased its sales to Walmart by US$250m, and Walmart dramatically improved its profitability on all P&G products.

The Walmart data exchange with Procter & Gamble has served as a best practice in almost all MBA and logistics courses since the mid-1990s. Dutch retail giant Ahold, parent company to supermarket brands such as Albert Heyn, Hypernova and Pingo Doce in Europe and Giant and Peapod in the USA, launched a data exchange program that took Walmart's idea one step further. Launched in 1994, the 'Today for Tomorrow' program at Albert Heyn (AH) supermarkets was aimed at radically changing the logistical infrastructure of supermarkets through an exchange of data with almost all suppliers.[30] Before the program, AH used at least 15 different logistical streams to stores, with multiple suppliers using separate order and delivery schedules. Some products would be delivered daily while others would not be available more often than twice a week.

In a single move, AH changed its logistical process to a fixed system of at least two truck deliveries each day, no less than six days a week for every store. To achieve this, AH guaranteed that key suppliers would be allowed to access real-time sales data from each individual store in order to track demand. They were allocated a minimum amount of space in AH warehouses and were expected to deliver the right goods just in time for the daily supply runs to the stores. The Today for Tomorrow program did not just impact the relationship between AH and one or two large suppliers; it demanded that the entire supply chain would work in harmony to keep stock in trucks and on the move rather than in expensive locations in distribution centers or stores. To this day, the Today for Tomorrow program is at the core of the logistical process of AH, with stores using significantly less space for inventory and the number of transport movements reduced by 75%. As of 2006, all suppliers to AH are required to work through the AH-defined EDI standard of electronic data exchange. Obviously, the best practices created by AH are now being rolled out at other retail chains in the Ahold group around the world.

Value Chain Integration for the Competitiveness of a Nation

The concept of Value Chain Integration does not stop at individual connections in the value chain. It has inspired the Dutch government and the Dutch logistical industry to embark on an ambitious program aiming to strengthen the leading position of The Netherlands as the logistical gateway to Europe. The key element in the program is the Neutral Logistics

Information Platform (NLIP). This standardized platform connects all logistical data from the world's fourth largest port, Rotterdam, Europe's third largest freight airport, Schiphol in Amsterdam, all major associations of transport companies and a host of other logistical organizations.

The idea behind NLIP is that all data about a particular transport is uploaded to the platform to be reused by all entities that deal with this transport along its route. So when a container enters a ship in Shanghai bound for Rotterdam, the cargo information, its origins and destination are entered into the system by the shipping party. Upon arrival in Rotterdam, all parties will use that same data from NLIP for further processing: customs, storage facilities, trucking companies and finally the customer taking possession of the goods. NLIP simplifies the entire process by sharing data between all relevant parties. It means less administration, more efficient planning, quicker handling, fewer inspections and a higher degree of efficiency in the entire logistics infrastructure.

The system is elegantly simple. But it took (and still takes) tremendous effort to get the literally thousands of companies lined up to work by the same standard in data. The system not only covers the cargo details and port of loading and port of call. Any relevant data about the transport is covered, from customs to hazardous materials, food and livestock authorization, rail planning, etc. NLIP is not a government program. It is a program in which the Dutch logistical industry and the government co-create. The aim is to improve efficiency in the value chain. Data Driven Strategy helps to cut the costs of complexity. Ultimately it helps to reinforce the Dutch position as the logistical gateway to Europe.

12 - Pattern 5:
Value Net Creation

Why sharing the same customer is a good reason to share data

The Value Chain Integration business model shows how data monetization is not just about selling data. It leverages the trend of the Connected Economy and uses data to bring organizations together around a common concept: the value chain. But even when companies are not in the same value chain, they still can find common ground on which to share data and achieve benefits. This is what the business model pattern 'Value Net Creation' is about. The predisposition for monetizing data in this way is the fact that companies are in the same value network. Or, to put simply: They share the same final customer. Exchanging data about this customer or his behavior can bring great benefits to all involved, including the customer, without harming each organization's competitive position.

In 1999, fifteen years after the first mention of the value chain by Michael Porter, Cinzia Parolini, professor at the SDA Bocconi School of Management in Milan, took the value chain perspective one step further and developed the concept of the 'value net'.[31] The value net, as the name suggests, takes a multidimensional approach to the concept of the value chain. Parolini suggests that multiple organizations form a network that can create value for the end user rather than a chain of companies creating value in consecutive steps.

In one of the practical cases in the book, Parolini describes how Italian coffee roaster Illycafè views its market for high-quality coffee. The company does not describe its position as a coffee blender in a traditional value chain but as a value creator in a network of closely cooperating organizations. The network includes coffee growers, manufacturers of home espresso machines using the ESEpads (Easy Serving Espresso) invented by Illycafè, coffee cup designers and specially trained 'baristas', the bartenders and staff who make coffee in hotels and restaurants. Illycafè has placed all organizations and functions that influence the coffee drinking experience of the consumer in a funnel drawing, with the coffee growers and producers of roasting equipment roughly at the top and the consumer at the bottom. From that value net it selected which functions should be controlled by them, directly or indirectly, and how it wished to cooperate with the others.

The value net places more emphasis on the 'what' and most importantly the 'how' of the value creation, as opposed to the focus in Porter's metaphor on 'who' creates value. In a way, in her book Parolini paves the way for Prahalad and Ramaswamy and their work on strategic co-creation. Where Parolini emphasizes strategic action to be taken by the initiating organization to cooperate with other commercial organizations in the value net, Prahalad and Ramaswamy suggest including the end users in the value creation.

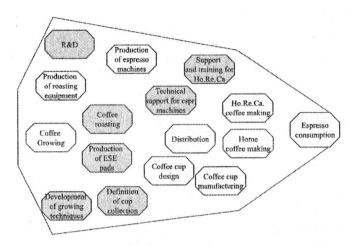

Figure 9: Illycaffè Value Net (Source: C. Parolini, The Value Net)

The Value Net Creation pattern takes the concept of the value net and co-creation one step further. It creates a flow of data layered on top of the traditional value creation process of multiple companies that serve the same customer independently. This data originates from the original activities of the various players and from the use of the final product by the customer. The objective is to design and leverage the data flow between all participating companies to the point where the data flow itself becomes a sustainable source of value.

As with the other patterns, the Value Net Creation pattern is driven by a particular source of value. In the earlier pattern of *Basic Data Sales*, the bank's transaction data holds value because of the analysis performed on it when creating the benchmark. In the *Product Innovation* pattern, the value originates from the data that is created by consumers when they use the end product such as the amount of money they spend on electricity. In the *Commodity Swap*, data holds value because it allows for differentiation of value propositions in a commodity market. And in the pattern *Value Chain Integration*, data held value because it allowed for cost reduction through smart logistics or an improved customer experience. In *Value Net Creation*, data becomes valuable because a group of organizations share data in the interest of a collective customer.

Value Net Creation in the Business Model Canvas

In the pattern Value Net Creation, organizations work together with one or more parties that serve identical customers and optimize the offerings to these customers or the process of serving these customers by exchanging data. The value chain is not so much a traditional chain but more a small part of a value creating system in the way Parolini describes it. The key factor in the Value Net Creation pattern is the single customer segment even though the initiating party is not necessarily the organization that directly serves this customer segment.

The Value Net Creation pattern combines aspects of multiple business models. In the picture above three different canvasses are intertwined by data. For reasons of clarity, some parties have been omitted.

The bottom canvas shows an airline using the '*booking*' activity (Y) to sell flight tickets to a '*consumer*' (A). The booking data is stored in a database and the consumer is made identifiable by a 'tracking cookie' in his browser. The airline shares its booking data with an advertising agent whose canvas is in the middle (left).

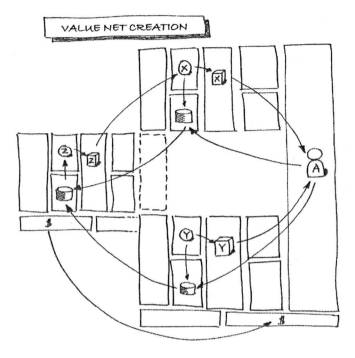

Figure 10: Value Net Creation canvas

The agent is allowed by the airline to recognize the consumer by the tracking cookie and search for his booking data in the airline's database. Based on this data and by the agent's key activity of a complex *'algorithm'* (Z), the agent can determine the data and destination of the consumer's flight. In the top canvas, a hotel chain is looking to advertise a product offering *'available rooms'* (X) to travelers visiting the cities where they own hotels. The hotel shares key resource *'room availability data'* with the advertising agent so that it can add this to its *'algorithm'*. The advertising agency then shows advertisements in webpages that the *'consumer'* (A) visits (through a partnership with website publishers, which is omitted from this example) immediately after booking the flight. The advertisements offer rooms in hotels in exactly the city the consumer is traveling to at the time he will arrive there. When the consumer clicks the ad and books a room at the hotel, a fee is paid by the hotel to the advertising agency and by the advertising agency to the airline as a compensation for the use of each other's data.

Value Net Creation: Adara, Inc.

In October 2013 I first met Tobias Wessels, the then newly appointed VP Europe at Adara. German-born Wessels is a Silicon Valley veteran, former CFO of Google's hush-hush ideas lab, GoogleX, and head of business development at Adara, Inc. in Mountain View, California. He had come to Ireland to lead the rapid expansion of the 100% data driven company. In a nutshell, Adara creates advanced customer profiles from data it receives from business partners such as major travel companies. With the permission of the data owners, Adara then allows other business partners, such as advertisers, to use that profile data for highly targeted advertising.

Adara offers a smart service that allows companies that share the same customer to target that customer. Multiple companies pool their data, and each reaps the benefits of that pool without compromising the privacy of the customer or the competitive position of either of the partners. Adara is a data intermediary.

Tobias Wessels' explanation of Adara's business model starts with a strikingly simple fact: 70% of leisure travelers make a hotel booking on the same day or day before they book a flight. For hotels and airlines, travel booking data is nothing short of digital gold. If only they could get their hands on that booking data in real time. They would then be able to place targeted advertisements on websites that this person visits within the hour after booking. That is exactly where Adara builds its Data Driven Strategy.

Airlines typically don't make any search or booking data available to any of their business partners. It would likely generate a lot of work, only limited turnover and the airline would have to deal with all sorts of different partners. Before long there would be plenty of travel agents, tourist attractions and car rental companies interested in the data too. But if the airline could securely license its data to a third party in a single transaction, and customer anonymity could be 100% guaranteed, it would be an interesting trade. Adara is that third party. It takes anonymized airline booking data and loyalty information, and through the airline website places a cookie on the travelers' browser. In the entire process, no personal identifiable information is captured, and all parties involved remain fully compliant with all laws and privacy regulations.

At the other side of their business model, Adara brokers advertising space for travel related ads on a network of websites. Adara recognizes the traveler when he visits one of the websites in its network and automatically places ads on these Web pages that offer hotel rooms in the city of the traveler's destination or other relevant offers such as car rentals or insurance. The system not only works on websites, but includes mobile and social platforms, too. It is a system in which all players benefit—even the traveler. Data partners, such as airlines, find new revenue streams, advertisers get access to highly targeted advertising to relevant consumer groups and last-but-not-least travelers get relevant advertisements and offers.

Adara has built a data driven business based on the data from multiple participants in its network. It aggregates this data and reciprocally generates additional data about the customer and his preferences. It uses all of this data to build a 'profile' of each traveler with the aim to offer both advertisers and travelers a more targeted service. It currently manages over 250 million profiles. The data partners retain full control and ownership of their data, but Adara controls the flow of data through its systems. It analyses it and extracts and creates value, and it allows each of these partners to use that value through its platform. A valuable proposition indeed, considering that only a few years ago the data was considered by its owners to be no more than an administrative byproduct.

PART III

PATTERNS IN
PRACTICE

13 - The Flipping Point

How flipping data from a byproduct to a core business can save companies

Business model patterns offer a luxuriously remote way of looking at implementing Data Driven Strategy. It is far easier to draw a model than it is to put it into practice. As mentioned earlier, making physical changes in process and proposition is not enough. It takes conviction, convincing, and extensive onboarding of colleagues and business partners. In the following chapters, I will demonstrate how companies have achieved Data Driven Strategy implementation, and I will elaborate on four important characteristics of Data Driven Strategies that helped them become successful.

When Google introduced AdWords in 2000, the company was looking for a scalable business model built on the added value of its search engine. Google at the time regarded itself as a search engine company. Perhaps some within the organization may have envisioned Google as a library, a publisher or a hub. And I'm fairly confident that at one time or another at least someone in the organization contemplated charging money to website owners for indexing their website in the first place. Google was in need of a way to earn revenue from its core operation: search. Selling ads would have been a great way to sustain the status quo. Google could simply outsource the placement of ads and offer the ad space to an advertising network. Meanwhile, Google could focus on its core competence—search—and make a profit. The AdWords mechanism, however, achieved quite the opposite. It created a system where turnover was generated directly from the advertiser; without middlemen, the world was the target audience and there would be sufficient ads to be placed on every search result page.

The system achieved all the goals Google had set out to reach but at the cost of its former focus area. Search was no longer Google's moneymaking business. The company had become an advertising platform. Search results had gone from forming the company's final product to providing its raw material. Google's customers were no longer the people who searched for information online and formed an interesting audience to advertisers. The real customers were now advertisers keen to publish their messages within a specific context provided by search data. Google had essentially flipped its business model.

As I have explained throughout this book, Google is far from an archetypical organization. But its transformation offers a very clear example of how organizations can shift focus from producing goods and services and selling these as a core activity, to using these goods and services as a lever to sell data driven goods and services at a higher margin. I refer to this shift in focus as 'the flipping point'. Depending on the volume and impact of this change in the entire organization, the flipping point can range from seemingly trivial at the product level to a strategic game-changing event.

The flipping point can be reached through each of the five patterns described in part two of this book. Even in a simple business model, such as the Basic Data Sales pattern, the turnover from data may outpace the turnover generated by the original product. Automatically, managerial attention will focus on the revenue generating potential of the data, causing the business model to flip. The company will manage turnover from data and treat the production of the original product as the enabler rather than the goal. Not a very drastic and an often unnoticed process, but a flip nonetheless.

Google's flip is an example of a classic Product Innovation pattern. Google did not simply sell its data; it created a new service using the data from its core activities. The company then instigated new activities aimed to generate more data in a similar way. From the outset there could be no mistaking when the business model flipped: it happened by design. Before the turn of the millennium, Google lacked a structural source of income and the creation of AdWords flipped focus from search to advertising. However, not all data driven products automatically result in a flip. When data driven products generate substantial but not noteworthy revenues, they may well remain little more than appreciated byproducts of the core process.

Over the past few years, many banks have introduced applications for online household expenses using the principles of the Product Innovation pattern. But despite their powerful potential, most banks have positioned these applications as 'nice-to-haves' and offered them to their customers free of charge. Lacking a solid business model, the products were never developed to their full potential and failed to become the data driven opportunities they could have been. This failure was not for lack of potential as the same products in the hands of entrepreneurs at Mint.com or Moven.com have become extremely successful.

More difficult than the flips originating from basic data sales and the intentional flip at Google is flipping a company's existing strategy. It takes courage and determination to leave an existing and well-known business model in favor of a new and unproven model. Moreover, it takes an extremely good reason. One such reason is current operations returning poor results. Companies in trouble with a bleak outlook turn to Data Driven Strategy to discover new revenue streams that allow them to leverage their existing core competencies and skill set. In the publishing industry, for instance, publishers facing decreasing advertising revenues can leverage their extensive subscriber base to collect data about consumer interests and behaviors.

Most publishers do not run into financial trouble because their content is bad or unappreciated by their audience but because advertisers are rapidly spreading their budgets over an increasing number of channels. Rather than spending their budgets solely on print and television campaigns, advertisers now funnel a significant portion of their expenditure to online and social media providers. Publishers can either try to follow the advertisers by developing their own competitive online and social platforms, or they can aim for a different budget within their advertisers business to receive revenue—for example, by offering services in product testing or customer surveys. Yet the market for online publications is highly competitive and the social media landscape consists of a few virtually impenetrable bastions. Not the best circumstances for creating new revenue. However, many publishers have succeeded in building excellent online versions of their original publications, and although these online versions often do not generate a large advertising revenue stream, they do provide a platform to collect and leverage data on consumer behavior. Additionally, these online publications contain valuable content that people may not be willing to pay for but which they do enjoy reading and watching. If publishers used the content from these platforms to generate customer preference insights, they could leverage their existing infrastructure and skills to build a new data driven revenue model. For publishers, to flip the old business model into a data driven business model does not require dramatic operational changes but, first and foremost, a change in mindset.

Commodity providers face similar challenges to organizations in heavily disrupted markets such as the publishing industry. They possess two core competitive instruments: price and customer service. Most of these providers share the problem that their products are of such low interest to their customers that offering excellent customer service is not sufficient to counter pricing competition. The only way to increase their profit margin is to offer additional services with significant added value. As I demonstrated in the Commodity Swap pattern, data is an excellent raw material for utilities on which to build those value added services. Providing electricity or gas offers a continuous source of data opening the door to the design of an array of new services. Contrary to the publishing example above, flipping the business model for commodity providers will likely take far more energy, perseverance and time. This is mainly due to publishers being able to use their existing infrastructure to generate consumer profiles that are more or less instantly useable. Commodity providers generate a stream of usage data requiring transformation into a particular service before it can be sold or leveraged. During my many discussions with professionals in the utility market, one theoretical example of a flipped business model has become the pivotal case for the Commodity Swap:

If smart meters, using the electric fingerprinting technology, allow utilities to gain insight into a household's entire energy consumption, the utility can offer a service providing a tailored, energy-friendly solution for household appliances. The utility could suggest a combination of appliances, such as a washing machine, dishwasher, refrigerator, microwave, etc., that best fit the household's needs and that uses the least amount of electricity. In short: If you install a smart meter, your power company can see how much power you use and which machines use it. Based on that knowledge, the power company can then suggest that you buy different machines that meet your requirements and that use the least amount of energy. However, asking consumers to pay for that data would not prove very successful. The logical customers for that data are appliance manufacturers, not consumers.

Utilities would benefit from servicing an existing customer base rather than changing its product offerings and its customer base, too. So if they cannot sell the customized energy advice to the consumer, they could consider selling the results of that advice. What if the power company flips its business model and gives you the power for free? Would you then consider paying for a subscription service in which the power company provided you with a washing machine, dryer, microwave, etc., for a fixed price per month with the guarantee of maximum energy savings (even though you get your energy for free)? For a growing number of power companies, the above is not a *fata morgana*. Many are studying the consumer trend towards access to goods over ownership (such as the trend amongst urban twenty- and thirty-somethings to prefer car sharing programs over the actual ownership of a car) and the opportunities it offers for their business model. By providing the energy for free, the energy company has real incentive to combine government pressure to reduce electricity consumption with the commercial driver to install appliances in the homes of customers that use as little power as possible to reduce costs.

Critics will state the idea seems wild and ridden with privacy concerns, and this is precisely why it illustrates the implications of flipping a business model so clearly. I don't expect any commodity provider to take such a single giant leap, but I know that many are drawing plans for a phased introduction of data driven services that may well closely resemble the above. The actual flip will happen when the power becomes free of charge.

Flipping the business model is not exclusive to companies in trouble, though. There is plenty of room for opportunity driven changes. In March 2014, Seattle-based stock photo publisher Getty Images announced that it would flip part of its business model, effective immediately, and provide 35 million stock photos free of use for non-commercial publications.[32] Getty Images is a leader in stock photography; it offers a database of millions of photographs for use in brochures, magazines, on websites, etc. Publishers and organizations are required to pay (by copyright law) for each photograph they use in a publication. Even though it is easy to digitally copy an image from the Getty Images database, the vast majority of commercial users pay for the use of the images. But an increasing number of private individuals were using the Getty Images photographs illegally on their blogs, websites and social media posts. Getty Images would frequently file lawsuits for infringement of copyrights, but they were constantly met with two key problems. Firstly, an estimated tens of millions infringements of copyright make policing the market practically impossible. Secondly, most private users would be more than willing to cooperate with some form of payment, just not the high out-of-pocket costs aimed at the commercial industry. Rather than enforcing a negative approach, Getty Images developed a technology allowing people to quickly embed photos in their websites, blogs or Facebook posts. Each time the page on which the photograph is placed is shown to a reader, Getty Images is notified. This allows Getty Images to make money in various ways. First of all, by knowing exactly which image is used where, the company can negotiate copyright payoffs with large online publishers such as Pinterest. It has become common practice for social media platforms such as Facebook and YouTube to pay royalties to copyright owners in a single deal to settle copyright infringements by individuals on the social networks.

Each year, YouTube pays millions of dollars to record labels to cover for any infringements made by fans that upload (illegal) copies of music videos. By enabling the exact measurement of the use of photographs on social media sites such as Facebook, Twitter and Pinterest, Getty Images can now legitimately claim turnover from them in the same way. However, despite its success, this mechanism does not flip the Getty Images business model. The real data driven value for Getty Images comes from the stream of data about which images were viewed on which website. Knowing that a particular image is being viewed on multiple websites is interesting in itself, but Getty Images has another trump card: It has labeled each individual image with metadata. Metadata describe exactly the type of image and describe what is depicted in that image. For instance, the description could be 'a businessman presenting to a group of colleagues'. The metadata add to this description by indicating that this businessman symbolizes success and that the people in the audience are holding tablet computers. If Getty Images can analyze which themes, concepts and ideas are popular amongst consumers, it can increasingly offer insights to those interested in that data: commercial organizations looking for consumer trends, scientists or governments.

Getty Images could go even further. By knowing on which sites a photograph was viewed, they could visit that site and index its contents. They could then examine the contents of the page and determine how the image was used to enforce the message of the article in question. That knowledge could in turn enhance the metadata of the image and create a competitive advantage over competing stock photo sites or make recommendations for the commercial use of that particular picture. They would even have the option to place targeted advertisements within the image. In the summer of 2013, Getty Images signed a deal with Stipple.com to research the concept of in-image advertising.[33] From the perspective of Data Driven Strategy, that cooperation may well offer a way to monetize the data within the image and the context in which it is placed.

As I demonstrated in the first part of this book, Data Driven Strategy is founded on the understanding that our economic environment is changing. Driven by developments such as the Connected Economy, the Internet of Things and Mobility, value is shifting to data driven propositions. When working on data driven business models, companies should not only set out to create new services, but should aim for a strategic shift: a flipped business model even when such a flipped business model is not feasible in the short term. A long-term vision, or 'Big Hairy Audacious Goal', as Collins and Porras refer to it in their book *Built To Last*, is not only necessary but must also be carefully managed.[34] For it is all too easy to forget about the future and get stuck creating data products that never manage to make a real impact. This is exactly where many Data Driven Strategy projects have failed to materialize as strategic changes in organizations. Not because they have failed to achieve their goals, but because they failed to change the strategic scope and direction of the organization. The reason being that projects remained just that: individual projects. As individual projects and products, data driven solutions are not likely to make a big impact on the bottom line, which means they don't get the managerial attention they need to grow. They do not drive innovation to the point where organizations take advantage of their changing environment.

Creating and offering data driven products and services without flipping the business model will ultimately lead to loss of competitive advantage because competitors who are focusing on Data Driven Strategy will be able to take control over the flow of data. They can focus on creating more unique data in their processes, create and control platforms for data exchange and co-creation and leverage economies of scale.

It is not necessary to flip the business model in a single daring move; in fact, in most cases that would be extremely unwise. Small steps are the way to go, but in order to actually impact an organization on a strategic level, each of the small steps will have to accumulate into a larger ecosystem of products, services, revenue streams and culture.

When we look at the patterns in Data Driven Strategy, each of the business models is impacted by four characteristics that facilitate the flip in the business model.

This chapter introduces each of these characteristics. In the following chapters they will be described in more detail.

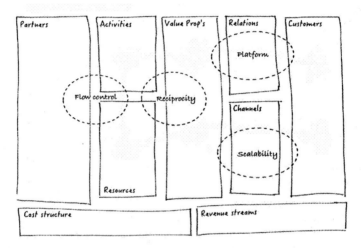

Figure 11: Key characteristics that help a business model to flip

1. Reciprocity

The first key characteristic in Data Driven Strategy is what I call 'reciprocity'. It is the effect that occurs when the data driven product generates new data the moment the customer uses it. The more people use it, the more data is being generated. In the Business Model Canvas, reciprocity originates from a 'key activity' delivered through the use of the value proposition by the customer and results in the 'key resource' data.

Reciprocity is what creates a consistent and continuous flow of unique data. In the Product Innovation pattern (see page 83), the online household expenses dashboard was configured in such a way that consumers actively add data to the dashboard; a new and unique source of data which competitors cannot duplicate. Reciprocity causes a flywheel effect that aids the impact of data driven products and services on the business model. Without reciprocity, flipping the business model requires exponentially more effort.

2. Flow Control

The second characteristic, flow control, is the discipline to create a managed, consistent flow of source material for the data driven value propositions. Flow control is managed at the intersection between suppliers of data ('key partners'), data management ('key activities') and the database ('key resource'). In the Value Net Creation pattern (see page 113), the managing company (Adara) controls the flow of data across the various partners, and this forms the critical success factor for the value net to work. It is what distinguishes opportunistic, and usually ad hoc, secondary revenue streams from strategically managed sources of income. The key words in flow control are manageable processes, raw materials and partnerships. These are minimal requirements for any successful business model and without them, no business model will flip.

3. Scalability

The third characteristic that helps a business model to flip is scalability. Data driven value propositions tend to have very different delivery dynamics than the original core products of the company. One of the key differences is the characteristic of data that it can be copied at a minimal cost without loss of quality or value. Another is the difference in customer base: data is usually aimed at a very large customer base. Serving a more 'liquid' product to a large audience requires a different sales approach and different distribution channels. In addition, data products are often used as raw material for other data offerings down the line increasing the pull on the data source. For instance, when a company offers its data to customers through an API (as a Basic Data Sale), it loses direct control over the scale at which this data can be used by direct clients and their customer base. However, in the early stages of data driven experimentation, when the impact of data driven products on the bottom line is small, most companies choose to use existing marketing and distribution channels to market the products to a small customer base. This may actually limit the success of the products as data driven products need to be managed for scale to leverage their full potential.

4. Platform

The last business model characteristic that facilitates the flip is the presence of a platform on which sales and customer relationships are managed. Data driven products, especially when served as a subscription service to a large number of smaller clients, usually are offered through an online portal or website where customers can register and purchase the data and where the data is actually delivered. In addition, the platform generally serves as the primary interface for customer service.

Data Driven Strategy requires a specific approach to customer relationship management. For most companies, the customer base is different from the existing customers, and these customers tend to have different needs for communication and interaction. Self-service, co-creation and networking are at the core of the customer relationship. Managing all of these different relationships requires a platform for both product and service delivery and customer interaction. In the Commodity Swap example, the utility company (see page 95) has the option to design and offer services and/or to create new services based on its data and sell them via the platform. The business model is not likely to flip (or 'swap' in this case) when the data service resembles the basic data sale pattern. However, when the platform increases in importance, the business model will soon flip to favor the potential of the platform on which value can be added in all shapes and sizes.

The following chapters explain in more detail how each of these characteristics allow business model to flip.

14 - Reciprocity

How to create a product that creates data that creates the product

The most effective Data Driven Strategies leverage reciprocal data: new data that originates from the use of an existing data driven product. Reciprocity in Data Driven Strategy ensures that value is created at the time it is being consumed. Reciprocity in data is everywhere around you; for example, in Amazon's book recommendations. When you purchase a book, the system uses this information to optimize future book recommendations to you and other readers. Reciprocity is used in TomTom's navigation devices: by signaling locations back to TomTom, the company is capable of predicting and reporting traffic jams and rerouting the users to avoid busy roads. It is used in Mint.com's online household expenses dashboard: whenever a customer enters his bank transactions or personal savings targets into Mint's application, the system is able to better analyze spending patterns and offer a personalized savings advice to all other customers.

Reciprocity is about the unique opportunity that Data Driven Strategy offers to generate raw material for your new data products simply by selling the products and having the customers use them. This is not an automatic feature. It needs to be carefully designed into your product strategy in order to work. But once it does, it creates a flywheel effect on data generation. Reciprocity creates unique data that none of your competitors can purchase and drives unique customer loyalty.

Reciprocity Drives Amazon's Recommendations

In 1994, Jeff Bezos, the founder of Amazon.com, was an employee at Wall Street hedge fund D.E. Shaw & Co, responsible for one of its high-profile trading businesses. During the quick rise of the Internet, David Shaw and Bezos frequently discussed the opportunities that the Internet had to offer them. They were looking for new businesses to launch and researched several opportunities. One of their ideas was an 'everything store', an online retailer selling literally everything. The store's website would act as an intermediary between manufacturers and customers. The company itself would never own or hold inventory, so it could offer an unlimited selection of goods to choose from. One of the key elements of this concept lay in customers' evaluations and recommendations of the products they bought. In the end, the 'everything store' turned out to be rather impractical to launch, and so Bezos opted to start out with one product category: books. Little did he realize then that the company he was about to launch, Amazon.com, would turn out to become the closest thing possible to the 'everything store' he and David Shaw had imagined years before. Or that evaluations and recommendations of customers would become the key driver of success for the company.

By 1997, the Amazon web store was already highly successful and turnover was rising sharply. But Amazon's mission statement included an element that it did not yet practice: it claimed that Amazon.com should be 'the most customer-centric company where people can find and discover everything they want to buy online'. At that time, the 'discovery of new items to buy' relied primarily on the evaluations of customers and the recommendations of a team of professional editors. The editorial staff was experienced and qualified but found it difficult to leverage the 'long tail' of all available books, supposedly one of the key success factors of the Amazon concept.

The long tail, a concept introduced by Chris Anderson in his book of the same name, includes the vast majority of books in Amazon's collection of which only a few copies are sold every year.[16] The idea that Amazon.com could sell all books (and not just the popular ones) was a discriminating factor in the success formula, but for the editorial staff it meant taking into account thousands of books that they themselves had not read. In addition, sales at Amazon were growing at such a rate that human resources among the editorial staff proved insufficient to cope with the rapid growth of the company. An automated system was needed to create the body of customer recommendations.

The website's first recommendation system was called BookMatcher and required customers to review up to 20 books or more to generate good recommendations. Yet even when those numbers were reached, the system proved ineffective. Recommendations always favored bestsellers and not the long tail of lesser-known books that would result in real discoveries, and worst of all, the BookMatcher system was not very reliable and would often crash when the number of users increased. So Amazon decided to redesign its recommendation system and created a completely new mechanism that required far less data in order to work and offered much better recommendations including books from the long tail. The system used a number of elements to create a recommendation: the products a user had bought in the past, the items that were in his online shopping cart, the items that he had evaluated and liked, and all of this in comparison to what other customers had viewed and purchased.

The recommendation algorithm was called 'item-to-item collaborative filtering', and it worked (and still works) by customizing each individual webpage to match the preferences of and recommendations for each individual returning customer. It proved a huge success. From the moment the new system went live, Amazon started leveraging the bulk data from its online store and became a recommendation company rather than an online bookstore. The data derived from sales, customer browsing, evaluation and plain surfing had become the raw material for one of Amazon's core products: the recommendations that powered more sales, more browsing, better evaluations and more page views.

Today, some 30% of Amazon's turnover is directly generated by its recommendations. It is turnover that would not have been generated had the system not suggested additional or grouped purchases to users. The company also uses its recommendation system to order the results on people's searches to match their interests rather than to show a hierarchical listing of items in the product database. For Amazon customers, such use of data is an advantage; Amazon is likely to recommend them products that they like, saving them time searching. It is a reciprocal system: Amazon uses customer's preferences to recommend them items to purchase, and when customers in fact do purchase them, they are automatically providing more data for the system to generate even better recommendations. Shopping more at Amazon means a better shopping experience the next time around and better recommendations for other people. The reciprocity scales outwards: it doesn't just serve you; it serves all customers at Amazon.

Using Reciprocity to Generate Unique Data

When the relevance of the newly created data is carefully designed to amplify or complement the original data, the new data will act as a trigger for a new reciprocity cycle. Amazon's recommendations lead to a purchase that reinforces the recommendations, which in turn triggers new purchases. Once this flywheel is activated, it becomes difficult for customers to start shopping at another online bookstore. After all, the more they purchase at Amazon, the better targeted the recommendations will become. Other online retailers simply cannot beat that experience.

Reciprocity implies that at some point in your business model it may become unclear whether the core commercial aspect of your process originates with the original products or services you sell or with the data that they generate. Since you own the process, you can fully design the data you want to generate when the customers use your product. It is this particular data design that allows you to create a unique dataset by carefully designing the product in such a way that using it will generate just the data you need. To create a unique competitive offering, it is important not to generate as much data as possible but the exact data you need to create a competitive advantage. To paraphrase and extend the popular design mantra: 'form follows function follows data'.

Using Reciprocity to Create Customer Loyalty

Reciprocity has another beneficial effect on business: it drives customer loyalty by leveraging the unique knowledge of previous customer experiences to improve the next experience. Each time your customer buys from you, it improves the quality of the next purchase. With careful data design, that benefit not only has an effect on individual customers, but it extends throughout the network of customers. When used transparently, customers will realize how they benefit from their loyalty and choose to stay with you. Amazon itself found out in the year 2000 just how transparent one has to be to keep customers loyal. In May 2000, Amazon had been under fire for testing various prices for MP3 players in its online store. Seemingly random, customers would pay different prices for the same product. Obviously, Amazon would know why and how the price was manipulated, but customers did not and got angry over it.

In a time where dynamic pricing was not as commonplace as today, Amazon opted to issue a formal apology. But they didn't change their policy, and in September 2000 controversy erupted over a new dynamic pricing issue. This time, DVD customers found out that frequent customers actually paid up to US$15 more for a single DVD than new customers. The discriminating factor turned out to be the existence of a tracking cookie on the customers' computers. This cookie is a small file on a users' computer that holds information about recent purchases at Amazon. If customers deleted the cookie and then visited an information page for a DVD at Amazon.com, the site would offer the DVD at a lower price than when the cookie was still active on the user's computer. Hence Amazon was charging loyal customers more than new customers.[35] Amazon officially defended their actions, again, with the claim that pricing variations occurred when user behavior tests were performed on the live website. The explanation, which was thoroughly valid at the time, raised speculation among analysts that Amazon might be preparing to 'put a price tag on the added value of recommendations'.

Auto Generation vs. 'Asking' for Data

Reciprocity does not imply that a system is required to auto-detect and generate new data every time a customer uses a product or service. Data can also be added to the system manually or at the discretion of the user only. There is no good or bad choice between the two but rather a choice in effectiveness. Samsung choose a fully automated, sensor-based system of data entry when it designed the Photo Suggest feature on its Galaxy NX camera. Whenever the user takes a picture in a particular city, the camera registers the GPS location of the camera and uploads it to a central platform together with other information about the picture that was taken. It uses this data to analyze the picture that was taken and tries to find pictures by other users that were taken near the current location. Using maps that are displayed on the back of the camera, the Galaxy NX can guide users to touristic hot spots not because they are using an official tour guide but because other people have frequently photographed that spot. Once there, the camera can even suggest the best position and composition for the shot. The Photo Suggest feature is fully based on automatically generated reciprocal data. Another design approach would have been to request the manual input of favorite places, with the risk that users might have found that process cumbersome or even outright annoying. In a different setting, users could be equally put off by an automatic data upload whilst they would very willingly enter the data manually.

Business social network LinkedIn is particularly good at getting users to add new information into their system by hand. In the LinkedIn network, users essentially create a personal profile in which they highlight their work history. The profile is very similar to a person's curriculum vitae. After creating this profile, users can connect with other users in the system by 'inviting' them to join their network. The invitee can then accept this connection, which allows both users to see each other's network of business relations. The value for users is obvious; by connecting to as many people as possible, users are able to find detailed information on a vast network of people they may want to do business with and get easy introductions to them through someone they know. Users are motivated to endorse people they know for the skills they have. Endorsing a person takes no more than a single click, yet it adds high quality information about that person to the LinkedIn database. Endorsements are only one of many ways in which reciprocal data is added manually into the LinkedIn systems.

The basic service is free, but for more advanced functionality (and access to more information), various types of subscriptions are available. The business model of LinkedIn moves beyond value streams from subscriptions and ads. By continuously motivating users to add more information about their professional lives and habits, LinkedIn becomes a virtually endless source of human resources research. With close to 300 million acquired users in more than 200 countries (as of April 2014), LinkedIn offers professional sourcing and staffing services to organizations. LinkedIn knows more about the evolution of careers than any other company in the world, and this allows them to suggest new employers for people on the lookout for a new job as well as potential candidates for companies looking to hire. In fact, LinkedIn probably knows more about career paths of employees in specific organizations than the organizations themselves. They might even be able to predict which employees are likely to leave the company—a dangerous but potentially valuable thought.

Reciprocity is what makes LinkedIn tick. The moment users stop adding data to their profiles, the LinkedIn mechanism falters. This is why the company keeps experimenting with new features to collect additional data, both automatically (from Twitter feeds or blog entries) and manually.

Ultimately it does not matter how the data enters your system as long as it does. As long as the system is truly reciprocal and the information flow into it is continuous and uninterrupted.

15 - Flow Control

Why controlling the flow of data is more important than controlling its value

A s you may have noticed, none of the four characteristics of Data Driven Strategy—reciprocity, flow control, scalability and platform—are about the data itself. They are all about the way in which your organization is capable of providing a consistent, scalable flow of data that is easy to access and of high quality. From the customer's point of view, flow control is probably one of the most basic and important criteria: It guarantees the continuous supply of dependable data.

If data were a raw material in an offline production process, flow control of the raw material would be a no-brainer. As soon as your supply of raw material runs out, the production line comes to a halt. With data, however, sometimes the consequences of not providing (or providing only part of the data) are not immediately noticeable. Since a majority of the data is obtained through a production process not primarily aimed at generating this data, quality, consistency or availability of data are not naturally embedded in the process. Flow control is as much about management awareness and attention as it is about technical requirements.

Flow control guarantees that all data that is required for the production and delivery of the data service is available, of the right quality and reliability and from a consistent source. In that sense, flow control mimics off-line supply mechanisms such as supply chain management and supply oriented risk management. But in Data Driven Strategy, data supply can be much more unpredictable and reliable than procured goods in a traditional supply stream.

First and foremost, all potential hiccups in the internal data creation, storage and analysis need to be managed. The processes that are used to generate and manipulate this data need to be adapted to accommodate the new data requirements. That in itself assumes that standards for data quality— including timeliness, relevance, completeness, validity, accuracy and consistency, as defined by the IBM Data Governance Maturity Model—have been set and are being governed.[36]

Even when data driven products and services rely on external as well as on internal data, the data governance required remains the same. But when the products contain consumer generated data, such as the LinkedIn example in the previous chapter or social media content such as Facebook or Twitter feeds, these products and services need to be constructed in such a way that their output is not jeopardized by fluctuations in the acquired data from these sources. After all, these sources need to follow the same data governance criteria as internal data, but controlling them is an entirely different practice. Flow control assumes the operational and managerial skills to govern the flow of data from any source and the discovery of new or additional sources that may be relevant to the product or service.

TomTom's First Mover Advantage in Flow Control

In early April 2012, over 90 drivers participated in a project near the city of Helmond in the Netherlands with the aim to improve traffic flow on congested local roads. 'Project Contrast' would test a system in which drivers were notified in their car of the ideal speed at which they should travel in order to prevent congestion at traffic lights. The project sought to improve on the constant 'green wave' speed advice, which on congested roads would lead drivers to arrive at a traffic light too soon and made them brake for the queued cars just before the light went green. By making the speed advice dynamic, dependent on the length of the queue at a particular traffic light, queues could be minimized, saving time, fuel (and pollution) and irritation.

The project was initiated by the Dutch government and integrated technologies from various vendors. Imtech, market leader in Europe for traffic automation, managed the (already existing) traffic light and road camera systems, national research institute TNO was responsible for application development of the advice apps for tablets and mobile phones. Global leader in portable navigation devices TomTom would not only provide the necessary hardware, but it would also provide 3G communications and oversee the project management. The project was a huge success. It proved that by showing people what speed to drive to avoid ending up in a traffic jam, drivers would in fact adjust their speed. In the process they would relieve congestion, save fuel and reduce CO_2 emissions by 7%. All without losing time.

When reading the case study carefully, one might find it odd that TomTom, the manufacturer of navigation hardware, would participate in this project in the role that it did. After all, TNO was responsible for the apps that calculated and displayed the ideal speed, and Imtech handled the entire road-based hardware and software. TomTom did create custom-made navigation devices on which the ideal speed was displayed to the driver, but developing and testing that new feature could hardly have been the reason to lead this project. It wasn't. Although the company did not make any formal statement about its reasons for participation, it is obvious that TomTom is keen to be the first to learn which type of data will be used in traffic-related communications. The company is permanently on the lookout to guarantee first access to traffic-related data so it can leverage this functionality and influence standards where possible.

Over the last few years, navigation device manufacturers like TomTom have been shifting their focus from hardware and software to data. Competition on devices has increased tremendously, and much of the navigational functionality has moved from the purpose-built device to smartphones and tablets. The effects of this on hardware sales are devastating. In its peak year of 2008, TomTom sold well over 900,000 devices. By 2013 the company was not selling even half of that.

In the area of navigation software, competition has also forced manufacturers to find other means of creating unique value.

Free navigation software, such as Google Maps and Apple Maps, has had a major impact on the profitability of navigation device manufacturers. So TomTom is actively expanding its service offerings in areas where it can add long-term unique value, and data is the driver behind that value. Years ago, TomTom pioneered systems for traffic information and joined forces with Vodafone to detect and predict traffic jams and reroute drivers along quieter roads to get them to their destinations quicker. Since then, the 'TomTom Traffic' service (originally launched as 'HD Traffic') has proved a big success and to this day remains difficult to copy. At its core, the Traffic system uses data from Vodafone SIM cards to detect traffic jams by counting the number of SIM cards registered at receiver masts along highways. Initially, the system was based on the number of mobile phones using a Vodafone subscription.

Today, TomTom devices that offer the Traffic service are equipped with a Vodafone 'machine 2 machine' SIM card, which cannot be used to make phone calls but which allows traffic data to be sent back and forth to the device regardless of the country in which the device is located at no extra cost to the user. Based on the data flow that TomTom and Vodafone co-created, and undoubtedly inspired by 'Project Contrast', on September 4th 2013, TomTom announced the 'Jam Ahead Warning' feature in its Traffic service. Jam Ahead Warning pinpoints the precise location of a traffic jam and sends an early warning alert to drivers so that they can safely reduce their speed. By controlling the flow of data from its own and third party systems, TomTom remains the leading player in traffic information and navigation technology.

Flow Control Requires Business Continuity

Flow control is primarily a managerial value driver. It shows great similarity with supply chain management and the need for supply chain resilience. The vast majority of data sales will take place as a subscription service, with customers receiving new, up-to-date data sets every fixed period of time. That requires continuity in the data supply. Yet even though most processes in an organization seem continuous, they are interrupted more often than first expected. In a report by the Centre for Logistics and Supply Chain Management of Cranfield University in the United Kingdom, the authors discuss a case study in which managers are asked the reasons for supply chain vulnerability.[37] The result of this study was that these risks more often than not were from the consequences of other well-intentioned initiatives. An example of such a consequential risk is the interruption of the supply chain due to another party attempting to optimize the process from a different perspective.

Similar to the example in the supply chain, cause and effect can have a severe impact on the continuity of data flow. Especially when people are not aware that data is a commercial product sold by the company. Earlier in this book (see page 80), I described an example of a company selling analytical data from its machines about molding temperatures, material density and flow resistance back to the raw materials provider. To keep production up to speed, backup machines would be used whenever a machine came offline for maintenance, but these backup machines failed to deliver consistent data for the new data driven product. Data continuity was lost every time a machine went offline for repairs of maintenance. Data continuity is the process to safeguard the consistent flow of data to the systems where the data is transformed into a product. Just as in any other production process, continuity in raw material flow is a minimum requirement for success and demands process and management.

Flow control implies not only control over the continuity and quality of the data, but also over the actual content. It entails that the organization should constantly be on the lookout for new or alternative data sources for current solutions and for initiatives that may impact current service offerings. When TomTom was first invited to participate in Project Contrast, it may not have been instantly obvious why a manufacturer of would participate in a rather small technology concept aimed at reducing congestion at traffic lights. The participation in the project allowed TomTom to test the flow of data from third party sources in its navigation devices. However, TomTom did not merely gain access to the data flow coming from the project. It gained access to a testbed for data exchange between road infrastructure and commercial navigation service providers. A position from which it can learn about, and potentially even influence, a European standard for road infrastructure data exchange. That position would allow TomTom to control the data flow and quickly scale the application of that data into its products and services.

Flow Control Creates Competitive Advantage

It is a popular belief that open standards, open technology and open data allow anyone access to all data, but this is far from the truth. Even though a formidable amount of data is freely accessible, it is hardly surprising that a thing of obvious value is not available for free; in fact, it may not even be available to the highest bidder. Data is no exception. Flow control not only assures an organization that it can obtain the right data; it also assures that some others cannot obtain or access it, or a specific part of it. When a company has full control over the flow of data into its systems, this enables it to create a competitive advantage and high entry barriers for competing products into that market.

When Adara started in 2005, the company secured first-hand access to some of the world's leading airline booking data. Based on this data, it built a data driven, game changing marketing platform. The airline data that Adara uses is at the core of airlines' competitive nature; this is not data they are willing to share easily. By managing their data supply relationship very carefully and delivering on their promise to build and maintain a profitable business based on that data, Adara ensures that no competing organization has easy access to the same 'raw material' that they have procured.

Strategic Value of Flow Control

In a few years' time, TomTom has undergone a transformation from a manufacturer of portable navigation devices to a controller of data flows, leveraging the devices and software as a platform to collect and publish data. The partnership with Vodafone is important because it allows the company to take data out of the device in real-time and to send new data to it. The ability to collect the GPS data from mobile devices puts a valuable data flow in the hands of TomTom. The company uses this data to provide drivers with innovative features in their navigation devices, and it brings the company extensive knowledge and data on traffic behavior and road usage. This data is valuable to a great number of organizations in, for instance, logistics, road infrastructure and government. In addition, the data collected from traffic also helps TomTom improve the data depth and quality of its business-to-business products such as location-based services, fleet management and an online portal with historic travel data called Trafficstats (trafficstats.tomtom.com).

With the navigation devices and their applications being transformed into a platform in which value added data services are being rolled out, TomTom is focusing on bringing in more data. The Traffic service becomes more accurate when more people use TomTom devices, and inevitably the company will want to see as many devices installed as possible. This will enhance the quality and leading position of their services and offer the best proposition on existing and future services to their customers. In order to secure the data flow of traffic data, TomTom may well choose to lower its hardware and software prices, and in fact it is not unthinkable that in future the devices themselves will be given away for free when signing up to a Traffic services subscription.

The focal point in TomTom's business model is flipping from manufacturing and selling devices to collecting and offering data based services. It is not a 'big bang' or a revolution—more a rapid evolution, but an evolution nonetheless. So we can expect TomTom to be on the lookout for more data in more areas. If the company can secure a leading role in data flow in other areas than traffic prediction, TomTom will become the most attractive choice for business partners and customers alike.

16 - Scalability

How scalability drives focus on sustained performance and profit

Data Driven Strategy is about creating sustainable value from the data that originates from your organization's primary process or products to the extent that it may become indistinguishable if the data is a byproduct from a primary process or if that process exists in order to generate data. That value increases incrementally with scale. For instance, for a company like Samsung knowing the viewing preferences and GPS locations of 10,000 customers is valuable for market research. This data can statistically validate preferences of customers groups about new features of televisions and cameras and similar research topics. This data, however, could not improve recommendations to other users or connect devices. Knowing the viewing preferences and GPS locations of 1 million customers around the world would probably allow Samsung to segment user groups and provide basic recommendations. But the potential products created from this data would not be overwhelmingly impressive. However, knowing the viewing preferences and locations of 100 million people would make it possible to co-create specialized TV shows with publishers, allow Samsung to sell data to tourist offices around the world and offer consumers not only recommended places to photograph, but also offer them special deals for local restaurants and theaters. It would make Samsung's Smart Hub platform interesting enough for developers to create and deploy apps, with Samsung taking a share in the revenue. It would, in fact, put Samsung right into competition with existing platforms including Apple's iTunes. But with a far larger number of devices connecting to the Hub, the value of the devices increases *and* it generates more data for the platform along the way.

In 2012, Samsung claimed it was selling three television sets per second, amounting to 95 million televisions in total. Research agency NextMarket estimated that in that same year, 67 million Smart TVs were sold across all brands.[38] In 2013, they estimate a total of 87 million sales and in October 2013, Chinese Xiaomi sold its stock of 3000 47" Smart TVs in just under two minutes.[39] Some are convinced that the 'second screen' (where consumers use a mobile device such as a phone or tablet to interact with their television) will beat the Smart TV hype. Regardless, the numbers add up to the same conclusion: an increase in data collection.[38] Remember, the focus is not the device but the data it collects. The more devices are connected to the platform, the more data is being generated—if not through the use of a Smart TV, then via a tablet of phone. It is a system that can be endlessly scaled.

Scalability implies that monetizing data from your current primary process requires careful consideration and a clear focus on scaling up usage. This is where Data Driven Strategy stands out from data commercialization. In January 2013, Gartner's Douglas Laney, VP of research and inventor of the term 'Big Data', predicted that by 2016 30% of businesses will monetize their information assets directly.[40] However, rather than 'trading, bartering or outright selling' as Laney predicts, Data Driven Strategy assumes careful planning and necessary alterations to both the primary process and the data infrastructure to maximize value. For some organizations, the changes required to become scalable are significant, but ultimately the rewards are clear for both the data vendors and their potential customers.

Scaling Beyond Expected Boundaries

Earlier in this book I argued that data sparks creativity in the most unexpected of places. The opportunities for co-creation increase when data scales to very broad and large datasets—not only by offering more historic data, but also by offering a broader scope. In 2009, Volvo Construction Equipment, worldwide leader in excavation equipment and heavy-duty loaders and haulers, announced it would equip all of its machines with CareTrack, a GPS-enabled machine monitoring system. CareTrack allows machine fleet owners to monitor their equipment from a single web portal. The data collected includes geo-location and a range of machine diagnostics such as fuel consumption, hours of operation, speed and approaching service intervals. CareTrack has been a success since its launch, especially with customers that own a large fleet of equipment such as rental companies. But Volvo has only scratched the surface of the opportunities CareTrack can offer. In order to maximize the myriad of opportunities CareTrack brings with it, Volvo must be able to offer more data to more customer types. It should be able to expand the number of diagnostics points in each vehicle. In the future, customers will likely want to monitor tire pressure, load per lift, angle of operation, etc. That functionality will likely cause new customer segments to emerge that find use in this data such as project managers working with various equipment owners in a single construction site wanting to tap into the data from various fleets and compare data on performance and project planning by measuring loads transported per equipment owner.

When I spoke with Volvo dealers and users, they all regarded CareTrack as a great system and acknowledged its potential for future expansion. The recurring complaint, however, was that no client used Volvo equipment exclusively. Other equipment brands are used in combination with Volvo machines, and they too use some type of diagnostics data system. That means that in order to gain insight into the performance of different vehicles, fleet owners and site managers need to collect information from different systems. A company like Volvo can potentially solve this problem using Data Driven Strategy if it can adapt its system to collect and use the data from competing brands within its CareTrack system. Not only could it gain insight into the real world performance of its competitor's products, but it would allow the company to scale its data beyond the known usage of today and accommodate creative co-creation and product expansion.

But scaling up to include data from other, competing vendors brings with it its own challenges. First and foremost is the question of why Volvo would want to spend time and energy enabling customers to add data from competing machines within its own software. This question drives straight to the heart of the matter: if CareTrack is viewed as an add-on feature to the machines, then scalability is not an issue. However, if the company recognizes CareTrack as a means to gain access to performance measurements of competing machines in the field, then scalability becomes a whole new strategic issue.

Scalability to Create High Barriers to Entry

When Philips and Sony were battling for the standard in VCRs in the 1980s, it was not a battle based on image quality or superiority in technology. It was a battle for market share. Philips sold a standard cassette type called VCC, and Sony's system was called VHS. The first company to achieve a decisive market share would set the de facto standard in technology. Not due to the inherent quality of the system, but because it would become the default cassette type for video rental stores. Rental stores have always preferred stocking one type of cassette, so whichever system boasts the biggest selection of movies would have the advantage. The biggest selection would drive sales for that type of machine, creating a very high entry barrier for a different type of cassette.

The same mechanism applies in Data Driven Strategy: the organization that offers the broadest dataset on a particular topic will likely be the standard that others work with. Scalability is key within that approach; even though your organization may start monetizing small amounts of data, this data should be scalable to accommodate new types of use and new customer groups. The ability to scale quickly can create high entry barriers for competing offers.

In line with the earlier example from Volvo, expanding CareTrack to include data from multiple manufacturers would create numerous options to become the leading benchmark platform. Volvo could visualize individual machines' behavior against the market average—for instance, in fuel consumption, wear and tear, etc.—because it would hold the largest amount of data from various machines. Each individual competitor trying to leverage a brand-specific system would be at a disadvantage from the outset as they lack access to all this data. Once customers have all of their data stored in the CareTrack system, they will find it difficult to switch provider. The focus on scalability for data (rather than the initial functionality of the software) will indeed have created a competitive advantage.

17 - Platform

How platforms drive innovation and keep you in sync with your customers

Monetizing the data from your Data Driven Strategy is not about turning data into bite-sized products and selling them. It is about valuing your data, building value-added products within your own markets and selling (or licensing) your data to others who create additional products beyond your organization's scope and expertise. A platform ensures that your company's offering stops at the point where it cannot offer any additional value. It creates a single body of data that is easy to maintain and distribute and is equally manageable for all third parties.

When Chinese technology start-up Xiaomi emerged in 2010, it set out to make consumer electronics with the best user experience possible. Quickly after the release of its first products in 2011 the company was being compared to Apple, inspired by the design of its products, the instant loyalty of its fan-base and the similarities between Apple's Steve Jobs and Xiaomi's president Lei Jun. From the early days of the company's existence, Lei Jun has made it clear that Xiaomi is not just about great products, but about the community and platform that connects all of its products and customers. Xiaomi is quickly disrupting the Chinese mobile phone market by selling its high fashion, high specs products at a very low price. The company's business model is far less about creating a profit margin on units sold than it is about monetizing apps and services. Lei Jun, who has been fighting the comparison to Steve Jobs, is taking every opportunity to point out how his company is different from Apple. In an interview with Dow Jones' technology website AllThingsD.com, Lei stated, 'I believe we are more similar to Amazon because we are actually using the hardware to build a software platform.' [41] To underline the importance of the platform, he pointed to the introduction of Xiaomi's 47" Smart TV and the interconnectivity of the devices: 'Smart TVs are the ultimate smartphone accessories'. With the standardized interoperability of devices, Xiaomi is creating a competitive platform for companies such as Apple and Samsung. Although the company has a long way to go to challenge the market dominance of the two multinational leaders, it has a business model built from the ground up that hinges on selling services through a platform with low cost devices supplying the raw material: data.

The Platform as a Single Point of Distribution

Data is the ideal raw material for any product: it replicates without loss of quality, it never runs out of stock and it stores for an indefinite period of time without losing its features. However, most organizations store their operational data in a location that is far from perfect for the role of 'warehouse'. They store it in 'production databases' that link directly to their core processes. Production databases are not very suitable as the key storage facility for data that is intended to be replicated to a large number of individual customers. Another storage facility for data that is available in most organizations, the 'data warehouse', suggests by its name that it is far more suitable for storing and replicating data. In many cases it is. But in organizations that rely heavily on their data warehouse for data exchange between applications or management reporting, even the data warehouse is not the right place. If the data warehouse acts as the primary source for data to third parties (clients or resellers) a period where sales of data spike might have a serious impact on the exchange of data internally.

By creating a single platform that holds the data and offers various options for its customers to extract the data they need from that platform, the platform becomes the single point of data distribution. From that point your own organization and third parties can develop functional applications with that data in the knowledge that they all use the same standard input of data. Whenever your data format changes or new data points are added to the available set, these must be implemented in one place only, and the changes should be immediately available to everyone and in no way influence the performance of the running of the organization. A single platform keeps costs of distribution and maintenance of data low and on the other hand enables a workable management of changes for the data users.

The Platform as a Means for Managing Commerce

The platform, as the single point of distribution, also makes the measurement of who uses which data more convenient. It forms a solid basis for commercial transactions and offers various ways of automating the commercial process into a self-service system. This is important because in a scalable system, manual transactions quickly become the bottleneck to success. Increasingly, service providers for hosting platforms, such as Amazon Web Services (besides selling books online, Amazon is one of the world's largest hosting providers) and Microsoft Azure offer easy-to-use servers and database software as IT systems on demand. This type of service is usually referred to by IT professionals as Platform-as-a-Service, or 'PaaS'. These services are increasingly expanded through the offering of e-commerce modules and visitor and transaction analytics. Microsoft Azure especially underlines the growing market for data products by offering a specific 'Data Market' through which organizations can sell the data that they collect and host on their Azure platform.

The platform allows a single place for customers to log on and retrieve and use your company's data, sometimes doing so without even contacting your organization directly. Customers could be allowed to set up an account and subscribe to your organization's data services without any human interaction. They could be allowed to download data files, connect to an automated programming interface (API) that can be used to connect the data source directly to a third-party application or log on to a particular value-added service based on your data such as query and reporting tools. The platform would register every transaction as well as handling payments and delivery. In doing so the platform allows your Data Driven Strategy to scale almost endlessly.

Platform as a Launch Pad for Creativity

The aim for co-creation is driven by the idea that third parties are more likely to create more and better solutions for a wide variety of customers than your own organization can produce. With your data at the core, these solutions are managed and marketed by third parties, who are experts in their field. In the early phases of Data Driven Strategy many organizations walk into the trap of offering customized datasets to each individual third party that they come into contact with. Although it may seem that tailor-made data solutions are necessary to serve new and creative co-creation initiatives, in the long run they will block growth. Even a limited number of individual data exchange agreements can quickly become unmanageable when the data format changes or co-creation partners change their solution and require different or more data.

A single platform for data distribution allows focus on providing high quality, high availability in data, whilst maintaining a neutral stance towards individual solutions. This does not mean that your organization cannot get involved in the actual design and creative process (or even the marketing) of co-created products, but it sets a clear product offering independent from individual solutions. In the long run this will lead to more solutions on offer rather than less.

Nike+: Single Platform for Activity Monitoring

In 2006, Nike launched a platform that would that would go on to become a textbook example of integrating real-life products with an online community. It would collect more data about people's running habits than ever collected before. They called their platform Nike+.

Nike+ is a relatively simple concept that was initiated when Nike researchers noticed that more and more runners on the Nike campus were wearing white ear buds. They were using Apple's new iPod Mini, which was small and light enough to take with you while running. At the time Nike was looking for a way to get more intimate with its customers. They wanted to extend the brand of Nike beyond shoes and clothing to an 'experience'. Music had the potential to be just that missing link, and so Nike approached Apple to jointly create the concept of Nike +. Nike+ allowed the runner to connect a sensor to his or her shoes and a receiver to his iPod. Once running, the user hears reports on speed and distance via the earplugs. After the run, the user then syncs the iPod with a computer and the running data is automatically uploaded to the website Nikeplus.com. On the site users can then interact with the data and analyze runs, measure distances, plot running tracks on maps and share all this data with friends and family. Runners set goals, and Nike motivates them to reach these goals. Because data is visible to friends on the website, runners can set up competitions with people who they are not even close to in physical proximity by simply setting a target distance and comparing times. Runners did not have to wear special Nike shoes to use the Nike+ sensor. They could simply attach the sensor to their existing footwear. With little more barriers than the purchase of the sensor, Nike+ was an instant hit.

On August 31, 2008 Nike organized a worldwide run called 'The Human Race'. Every participant used the Nike+ system to track his or her results on the 10-kilometer distance. The race was simultaneously held in 25 cities including New York, Paris, Sao Paolo, Quito, Rome, Mexico City and Singapore. But there was no immediate need to be in one of those cities to participate. All runners logged their run on Nikeplus.com. Well over 775,000 people participated and left their data at Nike's website. There was one overall winner, local champions and plenty of media attention for one of the world's most successfully marketed brands. However the biggest win was the deluge of data and more to come.

Although runners were not required to wear Nike shoes to use Nike+, the concept certainly paid off in a big way. Between 2006 and 2009, Nike's market share in running shoes grew with an impressive 14%. And it made Nike one of the most knowledgeable companies in the running sector: by the end of summer 2013, Nike+ had logged just under 1 billion miles. Certainly, the Nike+ initiative was no lucky shot. Heading up Nike+ strategy and development is Stefan Olander, a Nike veteran since 1996 and the vice president of Nike Digital Sport. Olander nurtured the Digital Sports division from its incubation to a fully operational business unit and in 2012 recorded his experiences in his book Velocity.[21]

Since its launch in 2006, Nike+ has grown into a well-established and well-loved component of the Nike brand. The original sensors and website have evolved into a series of products and services including a specialized version of the iPod

Nano, a GPS enabled wristwatch developed in cooperation with TomTom, specially designed basketball shoes with multiple built-in sensors and a bracelet dubbed 'FuelBand'. On January 19th 2012, Nike released the FuelBand sports bracelet as a device to record a person's movements. It measures steps, distance traveled and time spent on the move without requiring additional sensors. Throughout the day it turns from red to green indicating how much a person has 'charged' it with his or her physical activity. Once on a person's wrist, it records all movements including non-sports activities. The idea behind the device builds on the success of the Nike+ sensors and website: people like to get feedback on their workouts and analyze the data of their activities. The Nike FuelBand does just that: it records all movements and translates the results into a system of collectible points called Nike Fuel. The bracelet sends the results of the measured activities to the owners' smartphone and to Nikeplus.com. Essentially, the FuelBand is a smart way to collect even more data, and Nike Fuel has been established as the unified measure of reporting for all Nike+ devices. Runners and athletes love it because it gives them detailed information about their performance regardless of the sensors they use. Nike loves it because Nike+ increased the data flow to Nikeplus.com significantly.

No matter how much data Nike collects through its Digital Sports division, Nike did not set out to collect as much data as it could. It started out with a genuine belief in the added value of the products to its customers. However, most customers had no point of reference for the innovative products the team at Nike had in mind. There simply was no alternative available in the market by which it could measure its potential success. So Stefan Olander and his team employed a set of filters as a mechanism to determine whether a product should be launched.

The first filter was the question 'Does it make athletes better?' The second was 'Does it have potential to add a million new members?' The third question was 'Would we use it ourselves?' Although some other filters were applied, these three indicate that Olander and his team were genuinely looking for premium and user-friendly products that inspired customers to improve their sports performance. The team was acutely aware of the potential of the data that could be generated by a million new members, but it could not be done without adding value to their lives before and after. Data Driven Strategy is not about collecting as much data as possible but about collecting as much data as possible with a clear idea of how to turn that data into value and most certainly without compromising on the original customer value.

The Nike+ system is smart. It generates data from its sensors, and that data generates even more data when users share and add their own content. By standardizing the data flow using nikeplus.com and a standardized format such as Nike Fuel, the company controls the flow of data. That allows Nike to scale the concept to the magnitude where it literally can allow a million runners around the world to compete simultaneously. To athletes and runners, the platform that Nike offers through Nikeplus.com and the related mobile apps has become an indispensable part of their sporting experience.

On December 10th 2012, Nike made the next step in growing its Data Driven Strategy. The company issued a press release inviting young startup companies to join an accelerator program. The aim of the program was to find innovative ways to leverage the data on the Nike+ platform and to expand the number of applications using that data. By June 10th, 2013, ten companies had finished an intensive 12-week period in which they were mentored by industry experts and Nike representatives. Nike provided mentoring, facilities, connections and support while the teams worked on their products and services.

The accelerator program resulted in a demonstration and presentation by the 10 startups to a group of venture capitalists and angel investors. The accelerator initiative was a huge success. The companies participating in the accelerator program were given access to Nike+ data and built viable products based on that data. With products ranging from applications to find and book workout classes that fit your profile, log your outdoor activities or inspire kids to undertake active games, the accelerator took Nike+ beyond its own boundaries. In fact, the Nike+ Challenge builds on a theory that Stefan Olander and Ajaz Ahmed described in *Velocity* in 2012: 'Without a platform to manage and nurture every interaction with its consumer, a company has no spine'. By providing extended access to the Nike+ platform to selected start-ups, Nike is in fact growing the platform for customers through third parties. They provide more services to more consumers who in turn will find more incentives to add data. One of the companies participating in this challenge, Geopalz, is actively selling more sensors, adding more data to the platform. Sprout at Work created a corporate wellness platform, connecting whole companies, and Chroma.io creates sensor-driven games, adding player data to the platform.

The challenge was such a success that Nike has rebranded it into Nike Fuel Lab and launched a new edition in 2014. If anything, it will fuel the flow of data to the Nike+ platform, thereby putting Nike in a very competitive position. In January 2014 at the world's largest computer electronics show, the 2014 CES in Las Vegas, over a dozen activity bands were introduced by renowned brands such as LG, Sony and Intel. These competitors to the Nike FuelBand will undoubtedly integrate with apps on smartphones and have beautifully designed web portals. But they will inevitably lack the data platform that will likely keep Nike+ and its partners in the lead for a long time to come.

18 - Quality and Privacy

Why the biggest hurdles to Data Driven Strategy are self-evident but not straightforward

Selling data to third parties sounds easier than it is. Companies attempting to merchandise their data run into several problems. Each of these problems may seem trivial and easy to solve, but combined they are the reason why a structured and continuous process for data management is required before any data can be monetized. Although the specific practical issues will differ per organization, most of the problems filter down to two basic problem areas: data quality and privacy. Experts in Enterprise Data Management will likely argue that there are far more issues surrounding data management such as data modeling, normalization, governance and stewardship. In turn, privacy advocates will claim that privacy is not a hurdle to Data Driven Strategy but rather a ground rule. I agree with both; however, it is not my aim to go into detail on all aspects of data management and privacy. This book looks at building effective business models for data monetization. Data management and privacy are issues too extensive to be covered as a side story to monetization within the context of this book. The following chapter is intended to touch on these pressing issues regarding data when a Data Driven Strategy starts to gain traction in an organization. I recommend that at such a time you dive deeper into these subjects or seek external expertise.

Data Quality

As I have shown before on page 79, one of the most obvious problems for data providers is data quality. Data from operational systems simply isn't generated with the aim to be sold or used by third parties. Data Driven Strategy creates a pressing need for high quality data. Data quality management is a profession in itself. Many business cases and solutions exist for both technical and cultural issues. They take into account all issues that are related to the quality of data. IBM has defined a set of criteria that has become the standard by which data quality is measured.[36]

Issue	Explanation
Timeliness	The data represents information that is not out-of-date. For example, no customer contracts have expiry dates that have passed.
Completeness	All data is present. For example, the zip or postal code should always be populated in an address table.
Validity	The data is available in an acceptable format. For example, employee numbers have six alphanumeric characters.
Accuracy	The data is accurate. For example, employee job codes are accurate to ensure that an employee does not receive the wrong type of training.
Consistency	The data attribute is consistent with a business rule. For instance, all birthdates should be before 1/1/1900.
Uniqueness	There are no duplicate values in a data field

Data Reliability

The recent popularity of Big Data and the availability of large quantities of data from external sources have made it necessary to include an additional criterion: reliability of data.

Increasingly, organizations use data from unstructured sources such as online forums and social media. Data obtained from these sources is ungoverned and can contain unsubstantiated 'facts' that may turn out to be untrue. One example of how unstructured data analysis can lead to unreliable data comes from an analysis of tweets and Facebook postings. The recent Big Data trend seems to be homing in quite frequently on the potential of the analysis of consumer sentiment through social media. By analyzing what people say about a given topic on social media, the general sentiment on that topic can be determined. Although it is not my intention to ignore this potential altogether, social media analytics is anything but an advertisement for data reliability. Apart from the fact that tweets and Facebook posts do not in any way represent a solid statistical cross section of any customer base, some of the sentiments found in them are interpreted as quite the opposite of what they express.

Sarcasm proves to be especially difficult to analyze for automated systems. In my consulting practice, I came across one tweet in particular that represented the point in case. The tweet was about mobile operator T-Mobile, and it was interpreted by the analytical software as 'positive towards the brand'. The tweet read 'Another day without connectivity...Well done T-Mobile!' The example above shows how basic interpretations, even when made by sophisticated analysis tools, may lead to false conclusions. Data reliability should not be taken lightly and be governed at all times when data becomes your core product. Keep in mind that data reliability is not just a requirement for data you use and procure in your own products. Your customers may require you to prove that your data is reliable for them to use as well.

Privacy

The bulk of data generated by the core processes of organizations are customer centric. Especially when the customers are private individuals, the data will reveal a substantial amount of personal details about these customers. Telcos, for instance, register who called whom. Utilities register who used how much power and when. Navigation devices register who drives where, and online stores register who bought what. Customers are rather sensitive to commercial organizations collecting data about them. Especially when they are unable to determine how much data is collected about them or how, privacy quickly becomes a big issue. Even when they do know what personal data is collected by a company, consumers are wary about the level of their privacy.

When companies start selling customer-related data to each other and it becomes obscure who knows what, the customer can interpret this situation as rather Orwellian. After all, what is to stop your insurance company from increasing your premiums if it discovers that according to your supermarket's loyalty card data you regularly purchase unhealthy food? And why shouldn't the police automatically fine you when your satellite navigation data registered that you have been speeding? Not to mention the risk of systems being hacked and data stolen or hijacked by criminals. Privacy is an issue not to be taken lightly. First and foremost because it causes severe problems for those whose privacy is compromised; these people may take legal action, but usually no lawsuit can undo these damages. From an organizations' perspective, privacy concerns are not just related to legal issues when harm has been done. There are some very pressing commercial reasons for privacy assurance to customers and the public.

Customers Want to Feel 'In Control'

When European payment provider Equens announced in the early summer of 2013 that it had started selling analyzed payment data to retailers and other third parties, it met with steep opposition from the public. Equens is Europe's largest payment provider, processing well over 15 billion financial transactions from retail and ATMs annually. There were some obvious customers for the data that Equens generates by processing these payments. One example of an analysis provided by Equens was a 'share-of-wallet' analysis in which it compared consumers' spending in one retail brand to that in other brands. But even though Equens never sold any personal data, the public felt not in control and put up a fierce protest.

Since they had no direct relationship with Equens as an organization, people simply did not understand what the company was up to and therefore did not trust the organization with what they thought was their data. Although Equens went out of its way to explain that it never compromised privacy, it was forced to abstain from selling the data products. A costly exercise that shows privacy is as much about the facts as it is about the feeling of personal data being safe.

Less than a year later, ING Bank announced it had plans to display targeted advertisements to customers based on analysis of their financial transactions. ING Bank is a subsidiary of ING Group, headquartered in Amsterdam, and is one of the larger financial institutions in the world. Although this may sound tricky at first, ING stayed well within the Dutch privacy laws. ING's plans to monetize data sought to analyze data from financial transactions to allow advertisers to target specific clients with advertisements on the ING websites. For instance, they would offer a DIY retailer the option to advertise to ING customers that had spent at least €200 in DIY shops in the last six months. No personal or transaction data would ever be sold to advertisers. Advertisers would not even know when or to whom an ad was shown, and the ads would only be shown to ING customers who had explicitly agreed to take part in the program. ING Bank had taken all of the lessons from the Equens affair into account when it developed the program, but it met with even stiffer opposition than Equens. Within days after its announcement, ING was facing consumer organizations, the Dutch National Bank and even the national parliament. Even though ING never came close to breaking privacy laws and in addition decided to use an 'opt-in' system anyway, it still touched upon a very sensitive area of privacy and left customers feeling not in control.

Adara, Inc. (see page 118) realized the importance of privacy for consumers from the onset of the company and took the opposite approach. It faces privacy concerns head-on and starts by explaining why their service is safe for all. Adara handles booking data from a large number of airlines and other partners, and it knows it will be potentially out of business if there is so much as a shadow of a doubt about consumer privacy. Adara publishes its privacy policy as one of the most prominent features on its website. At the company, privacy is not about secrecy; it is about being very clear and open about what happens to data and who gets to use what. No personal customer data is used or sold. Guaranteed. Just like at Adara, in any Data Driven Strategy privacy is not a requirement—it is a hygiene factor.

Start with Privacy and Work Down from There

Most managers I've worked with found it difficult to understand that for most data products or services, it isn't even necessary to use or sell data on identifiable individuals. Adara doesn't need a person's name and address to place its hyper-targeted advertisements on various websites. It uses tracking cookies that are placed on the customers' computer. The data about the person itself is never registered in any of Adara's systems. The company simply doesn't need it and to make sure no unintentional harm can be done, it has decided to not use any sensitive data.

In a complex landscape of systems and intercompany networks, it is easy to make mistakes or overlook the privacy consequences of a single decision. In 2009, Netflix launched the Netflix Prize, a million dollar contest in which teams of researchers were challenged to improve the algorithm for recommendations of movies by 10%. Each team was given a dataset containing 100 million recommendations from close to half a million Netflix subscribers. The dataset was completely anonymized. No personal details were given, but each subscriber was identifiable by a unique number, so the researches could see if one subscriber had rated multiple movies. Within two weeks of the start of the challenge, a team of researchers announced that it had successfully matched the

Netflix recommendations to movie recommendations given on the popular movie website IMDB.com. Statistically they could prove that certain recommendations given by an anonymous Netflix user were given by the same person that rated the movies on IMDB.com.

Since people on IMDB are not anonymous, the researchers could now identify individual Netflix users and their recommendations, breaking the anonymization of the Netflix dataset. The incident caused quite a stir because the recommendations provided insights into both the political and sexual preferences of the Netflix customers. One customer actually sued Netflix after the prize for violation of her privacy reasoning that, as a lesbian mother, 'were her sexual orientation public knowledge, it would negatively affect her ability to pursue her livelihood [...]'.[42] Following the lawsuit, Netflix withdrew its plans for a follow-up contest in which it had already announced it would include ZIP codes, age and gender of customers.

Paul Ohm is an associate professor at the University of Colorado Law School. Round about the time of the Netflix Prize in 2009, he presented a paper at the Privacy Law Scholars Conference in which he stated that anonymization of data can often easily be undone or reverted.[43] So easily, in fact, that he warns that any anonymized dataset that is useful for research, either by science or business, contains so much explicit data that it can be de-anonymized. To state a simple statistic: 87% of all Americans are uniquely identifiable by the combination of their ZIP code, age and gender. Every dataset that has been stripped of specific names and addresses but does include these three facts cannot be treated as an anonymous dataset.

Each organization should assess its own risks for breach of privacy and its adherence to laws in each of the countries that apply to it. But apart from that, there are guaranteed ways to protect the anonymity of users. For instance, by not selling individual records but selling aggregated data. No person could be individually traced when the dataset only states that 25% of people living on Manhattan's Park Avenue have rated the movies *W.* and *Brokeback Mountain* with three or more stars. Or by performing or initiating the desired action based on the analysis of the data without ever putting the data itself into the hands of the data customer. ING Bank may sell data analysis, but it does not actually provide its data to its customers. It sells the analysis of the data and then places a targeted advertisement based on that analysis on a website owned by ING itself. The advertisers will never know who sees this advertising.

Companies that successfully monetize data do not treat data quality and privacy as 'issues' but as a hygiene factor. It is not a requirement for success but rather a requirement for an operational business. As I've shown before, these requirements may get in the way of traditional organization of activities and even cross the interests of managers within the existing business simply because they impose costs and limitations on activities that do not require quality and privacy in the way that data monetization does. That is why, as the next chapter will show, many data monetization initiatives are developed not inside but outside the organization.

19 - Managing Data Initiatives

Why Data Driven Strategy is managed by the CEO but outside of corporate HQ

Data Driven Strategy is not a project. It is not a practice that is implemented in one powerful 'Big Bang'. On the contrary, the execution of Data Driven Strategy much more resembles a technology startup than an established, well-funded corporation. Data Driven Strategy, on most occasions, starts with small groups developing innovative products with seemingly feeble business models. It is about small steps, incremental innovation and incubation of initiatives outside the core company.

Data Driven Strategy Is a Risk

In most companies, data is a serious subject of discussion; Big Data, analytics, and visualization are hot topics. Every manager in every discipline knows of at least one way to make his or her work more efficient, more reliable or more predictable with the use of data. Or so we are led to believe by these managers. In fact, only very few of these ideas seem to come to fruition.

When the Big Data hype gained traction in the market after 2010, most popular articles in the media were speculative promises on the potential of analyzing large data sets. In 2012 and 2013, the focus shifted to either technology or a few compelling real-world cases. By 2014 the focus shifted again, this time to a more skeptical 'need for strategy'. Even though Big Data is in no short supply of some very successful examples, an increasing number of companies seem to struggle getting their data strategies to work effectively. The problem is not that Big Data—or any other data application for that matter— does not work. The problem is that data has a significant impact on the existing commercial and decision-making processes in the organization. Data poses a risk as it challenges the status quo. Three examples illustrate how this is the case:

The first example is in Business Intelligence, the art of reporting and analytics in organizations. The introduction of Business Intelligence created transparency and fact-based decision making in corporate culture. The ability to have dashboards and reports on every desktop at the press of a button had a major impact on the decision-making process. This was especially the case in organizations where managers traditionally had been basing their actions on experience-driven gut feeling. In that way, Business Intelligence has influenced the political balance in organizations. Even today I am confronted by marketers who refuse to act upon solid market analytics based on the argument that 'they know their market like the inside of their pockets'. The discussion of 'who is right' is not relevant. I myself am convinced that the data does not always tell the truth; rather what is relevant is that data-centric decision making requires a new management paradigm. All too often, data is seen and used as a replacement for experience and expertise, and although that is incorrect, for many it is enough of a threat to begin with.

A second example of how data driven initiatives do not work well with running business is what I call the 'bottom line barrier'. It starts with a general directive that any project in the organization has to lead to a particular return on investment within a given period. Usually, this period is short: 12 to 18 months. Anything with an ROI longer than that is considered 'innovation'. Many customer-facing employees come up with some pretty good ideas on the application of data driven products or services but have no way of calculating a return on investment. The ideas are usually outside of the current processes or impact decision-making processes. Validation of the idea up front is often difficult simply because there is no precedent, no frame of reference. This makes creating a valid business case and financial projections a nearly impossible proposition, and even if it could be done, it would likely take so long to develop the business case and put it down on paper that momentum would be lost. Daily priorities take over, only to leave the good idea to die an unglamorous death. A rigid focus on short-term return on investment keeps most data driven innovation from even being considered by management.

Apart from politics, there is a third reason why well-organized companies do not seem to venture into data driven strategies: efficiency. Over the last decades, companies have rigorously organized themselves around super-efficient processes.

Principles such as Operational Excellence and (Lean) Six Sigma have created highly efficient and productive organizations, but at the same time they have cut off the road to innovation beyond the efficiency boundaries. Any attempt to use data that is generated for any other reason than was defined in the core process is officially identified as an inefficiency and is therefore regarded as a threat rather than a (future) benefit. Even when on a strategic level people agree that the sharing of data may be a good idea and put it into operation, operational managers usually protest fiercely against the inefficiencies that are introduced in 'their' process that immediately affect their performance indicators and targets.

In short, Data Driven Strategies tend to introduce new ways of thinking and working that are more often regarded as a risk to the current business rather than a benefit. Data changes processes, and change implies risk. Most managers do not have much of an appetite for risk. This is exactly why so many data driven initiatives, usually initiated by small start-ups, are capable of disrupting well-established industrial markets. Amazon should really have been invented by Barnes & Noble. Spotify really ought to have been invented by the music industry itself, and Mint.com really should have been invented by banks. None of these data driven initiatives were developed by established market players because they imposed a risk to the current business model.

Author and philosopher Nassim Taleb describes the danger of this risk avoidance in his book *Antifragile*.[44] Taleb argues that organizations, in order to avoid fragility, tend to organize themselves in such a way that they can resist extreme influence from the 'uncontrollable outside'. If they did not, they would be fragile and weak. In order to protect themselves, they become resistant to change. However, Taleb argues that resistance is not the right strategy, since resilience is not the opposite of fragility, from which it is trying to save the company. The opposite of fragile is what Taleb calls 'antifragile': that which *thrives* on change. It is no surprise, then, that companies that manage for resilience to rapid change are being attacked and beaten by the *'antifragiles'*, organizations that have nothing to lose and have made it their business to rapidly change and adapt. One particular form of company that has this impact in established industries is the startup. Startups have nothing to lose and everything to gain. They will adapt to any change the customers may require in order to survive and grow. That is exactly why and how they disrupt the establishment. In one of his lectures, Taleb argued that 'if you have nothing to lose, [you should] take as much risk as you can, by tinkering and trial and error: it is much better than having a strategy and intelligence. The industrial revolution has started with tinkerers.' [45]

The Parallel Startup

There is no standardized formula for success in Data Driven Strategy. Each company will have to find out for itself where the value of data can be monetized and who their potential customers are. What starts the process is a solid conviction that data represents value and that monetizing it offers great potential for the organization. After this realization, a fair amount of tinkering is required to find answers to questions and subsequently to turn data into viable products. Well-established companies are not the ideal place for tinkering, which is why Data Driven Strategy is often best developed outside of the parent company.

Even when the new data products seem obvious extensions of existing business, it is not always self-evident that they can be incorporated into the organizing company. In January 2014, I spoke with Rogier van Ewijk, CEO of Terberg Leasing, a privately owned €350m (US$475m) car leasing company active in the Netherlands. Van Ewijk had just reviewed the results of the new data driven venture he had started the year before, Justlease.nl. It was his third attempt at setting up an online private lease company, and this time his hard work had finally paid off. Justlease.nl had exceeded its sales targets in the first year by no less than 650%.

For many years, the Dutch car leasing market has been dominated by business car drivers. Private lease proves to be a sensitive concept for the traditionally first-save-then-spend-oriented Dutch. Yet in a declining and highly competitive corporate leasing market, the incentive to venture into the private lease market is substantial. So after two unsuccessful attempts, Van Ewijk decided to take a different approach. He decided to not only create a new market for leasing cars to private individuals but to build it on the principles of Data Driven Strategy. He would be leasing out the cars with the aim to create a sizable database of traffic data and driver profiles. The ultimate goal was, and still is, to lease out the cars at a minimum fee, or even for free, and to use data as the primary driver for creating turnover. Data Driven Strategy forced the private lease company into a business model that differed from that of traditional leasing companies.

The first two attempts at launching a private lease product had been started from within the parent company. This product had been launched alongside the existing portfolio of the corporate lease products. It did not work. Seemingly small variances in process between corporate and private lease turned out to be much more substantial in practice. Private individuals turn out to be a very different type of customer to deal with than business drivers. First and foremost, business drivers do not directly deal with the financial consequences of, for instance, repairs and damages. These disparities quickly led to commercial mistakes, skewed focus and a loss of quality in both the business and the private lease products.

Within the same operations, the private lease products failed to satisfy customers and the impact on operational excellence in the corporate lease service meant lower margins and frustrated employees. So in the end Van Ewijk decided to launch the private lease product a third time, this time from an empty office across the street. He embarked on this new attempt with a small, dedicated team, under a different brand name and with a different operating model focused on data. His gamble paid off: the small team acted as real entrepreneurs. The company website formed the focal point of operations and was built by the company's own developers. It was built to collect and use all possible data about customers and their behavior, and it was not based on a 'grand design' attempting to mimic existing lease companies but by taking small steps and building on what proved to be successful in practice.

Sales boomed and data started flowing into the company. Van Ewijk and his team are brimming over with ideas to leverage data to make cars cheaper. They are experimenting with dynamic insurance, for instance, allowing people to pay different insurance premiums depending on the regions they drive in and location-based offers for gas or refreshments, using the driver's smartphones to communicate. Another example is offering tips and tricks for cheaper and safer driving based on actual driving behavior. The array of products even included in-car advertising. These kinds of initiatives wouldn't even make the conversation at the coffee machine in regular leasing companies. Implementation is step by step, and each innovation needs a solid financial basis just like any other company. Even though data is a high priority, servicing happy drivers is always the priority. However, the relentless focus on data and the parallel startup scenario are present in all decision-making and strategic choices, and this sets the company apart from other private lease companies.

Like the leasing example above, in Data Driven Strategy organizations tend to launch new, innovative products to new customer segments. In most cases, they face great difficulty integrating the new product/market combination into the existing processes and culture. Even if the new products have already been created, they are not easily adapted to the existing product portfolio and marketing calendar. However, in most cases the products are not even finished. They are at best first editions in need of field testing, customer feedback, adaptation and more field testing. Again, not exactly the right type of product to hand to an existing organization that makes most of its profits in a different market. The best place to launch this type of product is a startup. But not just any startup: a startup that can operate by itself, make its own decisions and tinker at will. One where sharing expertise, experience and resources with the parent company is best practice but not a birthright. A startup that knows that even though at some point in time it may integrate its activities back into the parent company, until then it is solely responsible for its success. Most importantly, it is the type of startup that gets its key resource from the parent company: data. I call this type of startup the 'parallel startup'.

Parallel startups are a proven way to leverage innovative business models from existing companies. Terberg, after trying twice before, finally launched Justlease.nl as a parallel startup. Amazon.com, itself a startup only 10 years before, launched Lab126 to develop the Kindle e-reader. Nike commissioned Stefan Olander to start Nike Digital Sport as a parallel startup. Many additional examples of parallel startups can be found in the music industry and in publishing. It is important to note that even though the parallel startup is an independent organization, the common interest between the parent company and the startup is managed for maximum benefit. A careful balance is required in the exchange of resources and expertise. This balance is maintained through three key principles:

Principle 1. The CEO Runs the Show

Especially the smaller parallel startups tend to be regarded by senior management in the parent company as a project rather than as an organization. Since data is involved, the CIO often claims the startup as his or her domain, only to have the leadership disputed by the marketing team, who see product development or business development as their exclusive expertise. And since the startup represents a high-risk investment, the CFO wants to have his say as well. Regardless of these internal politics, there can be only one person to lead the parallel startup: the CEO. This CEO will then need to appoint a leader for the startup who is fully determined to make his company bigger than the parent, a dedicated startup CEO capable of defending his own point of view against that of the parent's leadership. Rogier van Ewijk personally oversaw the developments at Justlease.nl. At Nike Digital Sport, Stefan Olander was trusted with the development of his own division and reported directly to Nike's CEO Mark Parker. At Lab126, the newly appointed CEO Greg Zehr took a small team of hardware developers to a Palo Alto law library to develop the Kindle e-reader. Greg Zehr reported directly to Jeff Bezos.

The reason for this strict separation is the inevitable conflict of interest that is going to arise between the two companies. If senior managers in the parent company other than the CEO are trusted with explicit goals and targets for the parent company, they will manage the startup in such a way that its activities will contribute to the parent's goals. The startup needs to operate as a fully independent entity, and the only leader who can set specific targets independent from the parent's goals is the parent's CEO.

Principle 2. The Startup Is a Co-creating Client

The startup will use data from the parent as raw material for its products and services. It is highly unlikely that the data source will remain unchanged and simply divert its data flow from the parent to the startup. This means that close cooperation between the two companies is required to create a reliable and sustainable flow of data. That kind of cooperation cannot exist in the parent company if no compensation is offered. Simply put: no manager in the parent company can or will devote the time and energy of his team to helping the startup if it doesn't help him to achieve his own targets. So the startup will have to become a client and pay for the services rendered by the parent. As any client, the startup will be serviced by an account manager from the parent.

In addition, the startup will likely have some very explicit demands and needs for the data it purchases from the parent, so cooperation between the two companies to create the right data source for the startup is required. The two companies need to co-create the final product. This requires a structured cooperation in the form of a 'data team' consisting of people from both companies. It is vital that this team adheres strictly to technical issues and leaves commercial decisions to the account team. Obviously, the cooperation between the two companies does not limit itself strictly to data delivery. Other functions, such as customer support, HR or procurement, can be outsourced from the startup to the parent company. However, a strict client/supplier relationship must be retained.

Just like any other client, the startup is kept out of the loop on developments in the parent company that are none of their business, just as parent employees are kept from meddling with affairs in the startup. Even when the two companies are in different office locations, the tight personal networks will likely keep the two closely linked, and each CEO will find himself policing differences between the startup and the parent. Keeping the boundaries strict is important because it allows the startup to develop itself independently from the parent company. In theory it would be possible for the startup to obtain data from another source than the parent at any given time. Since the startup pays the parent for the data, that will be felt immediately as a loss and thus keeping a healthy distance benefits both organizations.

Principle 3. Manage for Growth, Not for Split

The ultimate goal of the two companies is not to split the organizations apart. The reason to put the data driven business in a separate startup is to create an optimal environment for growth without disturbing the process of the running business.

At the launch of the parallel startup, the data driven initiative simply does not match the processes and culture of the parent company. But there will be a point in time when the startup has grown out of infancy. It will likely require more structure and leverage economies of scale. It could benefit from closer cooperation or even re-integration with the parent company, simply because that type of organization would accelerate growth.

CEOs must regard the parallel startup as a way to create an optimal environment to develop and grow Data Driven Strategies, not as a way to develop and grow new organizations. When aiming for growth, the organizational entity functions as an enabler rather than as a purpose. Employees in both the parent company and in the startup will stay focused on the maximum value that each partner can offer the other. Because of these benefits, Nike Digital Sport has now evolved from a startup to a full division of Nike. Lab126, although still separate from Amazon's offices, does not operate as a fully independent company but as a research lab for Amazon. Terberg Leasing, the parent company of Justlease.nl, takes this development one step even further. A little over one year after launching the startup, established teams in the parent company are looking at incorporating ideas and processes from the startup to improve their own performance.

Developing Innovation

Many companies recognize their limitations in innovative capacity: the political and cultural suspicion towards data, return on investment demands and efficiency targets. They recognize that their current business is all but the suitable environment to create and foster small and unproven ideas into viable and marketable products. In addition, in the wake of Prahalad's ideas on co-creation and the increased efficiency in partnerships through the Connected Economy, more and more organizations are seeing the possibility to develop these new ideas in collaboration with others. They are led and inspired by some impressive examples from companies such as Procter & Gamble. In 2000, when the newly appointed CEO Alan Lafley realized that P&G could not meet its growth targets through traditional R&D, he challenged the company to find better ways to innovate.[46] This resulted in the 'Connect & Develop' program, which aimed to work more closely with external partners to invent new products. Within five years, more than 35% of new products used elements that originated from outside P&G, a 20% increase from the year 2000. In total, R&D productivity had increased by nearly 60%. Today, the Connect & Develop program is at the core of innovation at P&G, and many of the companies that participate in the co-creation platform are in fact small companies.

In much the same way, leaders in Data Driven Strategy are taking innovation out of the core company and into the open market space. They do so not only to overcome the limitations of innovation that exist within the company, but also to leverage creativity, expertise and drive. As I explained earlier in this book, data is like Lego; it sparks creativity in other businesses. Open innovation creates access to just the kind of creativity that is hard to find within the existing organization. In the last few years, two popular 'weapons of choice' have emerged for data centric innovation: hackathons and accelerator programs. Although subject to trends and certainly not the only way to stimulate or leverage innovation, both are good examples of how organizations can stimulate an innovation atmosphere and environment.

Hackathons

Hackathons, a portmanteau of the words 'hacking' and 'marathon', originated in the Internet startup industry in the late 1990s. Although today still a peculiar phenomenon to most business people, hackathons are quickly becoming a popular driver for innovation in established organizations. In essence, a hackathon is an event in which competing teams of computer programmers and designers are given a data set and asked to develop a working prototype of an application using that data within 24 hours. In this way, a hackathon results in multiple working prototypes of software applications in a very short timeframe. From all products that emerge from the hackathon, a jury will pick a winner to be further developed into a marketable product. Obviously, multiple variations on the theme are possible.

The type of solution to be developed may be specified in more detail and the timeframe may differ, but the concept is that of a pressure cooker process leading to multiple possible solutions. The teams developing new solutions during a hackathon may be from within the organizing company but are more often outsiders. For instance technology startups, software developers, multidisciplinary teams and even well established companies are using hackathons as a means of business development. They subscribe to the challenge provided by the organizer for any number of reasons, but most commonly for the commercial opportunity or for the sheer glory that comes with developing a winning or runner-up concept for a big brand company. Hackathons do not follow a very strict format. Some are outright opportunistic and many are held online rather than in the organizer's facilities. Not too long ago, I visited a software company when they were participating in a hackathon that had been organized by a bank. The aim was to develop new ways of analyzing data for marketing purposes. Small teams of developers were scattered around the company's office and the adjacent cafeteria. They were working frantically on their laptops and iPads and communicating with the bank (and other competing teams) via an enormous video wall that had been installed for the occasion. While their colleagues were finishing up on an important piece of code, a team of developers who were waiting for just that piece of code was killing time by trying to find out who could slide farthest through the office hallway on a bright orange Fatboy beanbag. The event captured the exact spirit of most hackathons: a combination of relentless hard work, unlimited energy, creative inspiration and good fun.

Hackathons are extremely well suited to generate creative solutions to relatively simple problems or to quickly find value in previously uncharted areas such as a company's data. A hackathon opens up the creative arsenal of the outside world and leads to innovative solutions based on a combination of an 'outside-in' view and technological expertise. Hackathons also offer another advantage. Most companies that I have worked for in the field of Data Driven Strategy only had a very general idea of how the value of their data might be leveraged when first starting out. In many cases that idea was no more than a CEO's gut feeling or a CIO's professional conviction that data held value. By using the business model patterns I described in part two of this book, senior management could translate that gut feeling into an understanding of how data influences value propositions to customer segments. The exercise usually generates a number of practical ideas and applications for data along the way. But it doesn't translate these ideas into concrete products. Hackathons are very suitable for quickly developing various working prototypes for these ideas. For established organizations, hackathons are an especially good way to come into contact with creative startups and to test their capabilities and culture in the process.

Accelerator Programs

Contrary to hackathons, accelerator programs, or simply accelerators, take time to develop and build more elaborate solutions. Even though most accelerators result in new, creative solutions, they are primarily aimed at accelerating their implementation. Where hackathons push to get a minimum viable product in a short period of time, accelerators aim for a more thoroughly developed marketable product. The goal, in most cases, is to kick-start a product so that it can be launched almost immediately. Accelerators provide the right environment for innovation through capital, coaching and networking. Accelerator programs usually last anywhere between 30 and 90 days. Teams of developers, similar to hackathons usually coming from outside the company, have time to prepare and pre-develop their ideas. They are thoroughly briefed by the organizer in advance, and during the program they receive extensive coaching from subject matter experts, entrepreneurs and finance professionals such as venture capitalists. Accelerators have a well-defined beginning and end and tend to have a 'winner'. Even though most accelerators are organized by established firms that invite startups to participate, there are many examples of companies organizing accelerators for internal teams.

As I showed before in chapter 17, in 2013 Nike Digital Sport organized the Nike+ Accelerator, in which 10 companies developed innovative solutions using Nike+ data. The accelerator was a huge success, and as a result, Nike Digital Sport decided to continue the program. By 2014, the accelerator was rebranded Nike Fuel Lab and challenged another 10 companies to participate in a 12-week program. The participants were sponsored with US$50,000 and exclusive access to the Nike+ data and specific software development platforms. In addition, the teams received office space in San Francisco, access to Nike's senior executives and mentors and education. In this way, the Nike Fuel Lab accelerator has become the driving force behind data driven innovation for the digital division of the sports brand.

Accelerators offer an opportunity for established companies to connect to startups and to get to know them very well (and put them through their paces) in a relatively short space of time. Although far more expensive than hackathons, accelerators create not only a more developed product but also a closer bond between the two companies. Or, as Taleb might phrase it, continued access to tinkering.

Lean and Iterative Development

The emphasis in the last sentence is not so much on the tinkering but on the continuity of it as data driven products are almost never complete. New data will become available, reciprocity generates even more data, open innovation and open platforms attract new clients that build new solutions based on the data and they will require changes and additions to the platform. The Data Driven ecosystem is a constantly changing ecosystem which cannot be designed and built in one project. It should be managed as an ongoing process.

Hackathons and accelerators help to create an initial version of a data driven product. But the initial product is only the beginning. It must then be validated by customers, feedback needs to be collected and reviewed and changes to the product need to be made. This process is continuous and never results in a finished product.

Data Driven Strategy is not the only area in which the iterative approach to product development is used. The origins of iterative development are found in software development, where during the mid 1990s lightweight, iterative software development was beginning to emerge over the 'heavyweight' software development in which applications were designed and built in one major push. The lightweight development centered on developing small parts of a bigger program in succession, with rigorous testing in between releases. This allowed for the adoption of changes to the original high-level design based on user feedback along the development process. Today, iterative software development is the norm and has taken root in structured processes and methods, collectively named 'agile software development'. The importance of iterative development as a principle is underlined by Facebook CEO Mark Zuckerberg in his letter to investors, 4 months before the IPO. He calls it 'The Hacker Way':

"The Hacker Way is an approach to building that involves continuous improvement and iteration. Hackers believe that something can always be better, and that nothing is ever complete. They just go and have to fix it – often in de face of people who say it's impossible or are content with the status quo."

Hackers try to build the best services over the long term by quickly releasing and learning from smaller iterations rather than trying to get everything right all at once. To support this, we have built a testing framework that at any given time can try out thousands of versions of Facebook. We have the words 'Done is better than perfect' painted on our walls to remind ourselves to always keep shipping.[47]

When he refers to 'The Hacker Way', Zuckerberg is not so much pointing to software development as a process but rather to product development as a strategy. Zuckerberg is not the first and certainly not the only person to stress the importance of iterative design and development. One of the most influential books that have recently been written on the subject is *The Lean Startup* by Eric Ries.[48] In its core, Ries describes the key problem that entrepreneurs face when they launch a new product from a new company. The founders have a great idea and an enormous drive to succeed, but no product and no existing customer base. In Data Driven Strategy, the situation is virtually always the same. The parent company has a bold vision to monetize its data. The team it appoints to make this happen is highly motivated and ready to go. It may even have an initial product, developed in a hackathon or an accelerator program. But still it is created out of a vision of what is needed, not out of feedback from customers actually using the product. It is never a finished product but merely the starting point of a rigorous exercise to develop, test, measure and adapt to new demands.

Ries' core message lies in the fact that customer response to innovative products is unpredictable. There is no way that organizations can, in advance, define the way customers will use and like data driven products. That is why the best way to start is to build a simple version of a product, sell it to customers and listen very carefully to what they have to say. The simple version, or 'Minimum Viable Product' as Ries calls it, is basically a testbed for ideas. Based on the customers' answers, the product will be adapted, sold and new responses generated. A new cycle of development follows, and over time the product will develop in the direction that meets the needs of customers rather than the theoretical ideas of researchers and developers. The key measurements for success in the early stages are not financial but the value that customers see in the product and the rate of growth of the user base.

The product value is measured by the number of frequent users and growth is measured by the number of new customers purchasing the product. By keeping financial measurements out of the equation the startup is able to measure success in the early stages even when the early return on investment is poor compared to normal business standards. However, the non-financial metrics do form the basis for future financial measurement and allow the startup to decide whether the current direction the product is taking will suffice for future earnings. If the value perception is low or the growth is slowing, the company may decide to 'pivot' and pursue a different direction.

Case: Innovation in Smart Energy

In 2013, Marcelle Mettes was appointed as director of innovation and marketing development at Essent. With a turnover in excess of €6 billion, Essent is the biggest utility in the Netherlands and is responsible for over 10% of the turnover of parent company RWE Energy, one of Europe's leading energy providers. For the past five years, Europe's energy market has been in turmoil. Due to economic downturn, steep targets in CO_2 reduction and EU governments subsidizing green energy production (and local solar power generation in particular) electricity prices in Western Europe have been falling rapidly. This has resulted in a paradigm shift in each local European market. Like all other European energy producers and traders, Essent is therefore placing a strong focus on innovation to counter the irreversible downturn in its traditional markets. The Essent workforce has picked up the gauntlet and started several initiatives to develop and test new products and explore new business opportunities. Mettes, who reports directly to the board, was appointed to transform Essent into a more innovative 'eco-system' to accelerate and channel new business opportunities into viable and compelling solutions for customers. She wants to get there before her competitors take the initiative.

'We're in a market under fire. The current business model simply will not last. We need to change, there is no alternative.' But changing the mindset of a company with a long history is not easy. Especially for solutions that lie far from the current business model. 'The fact that we generate lots of valuable data simply hasn't occurred to most employees yet. Taking a single leap to Data Driven Strategy is not likely to succeed. Selling data-driven solutions is a whole different concept from selling energy. Yet the commercial pressure is on. We need quick wins and easy to understand customer solutions first, such as the e-Thermostat. In addition we are investing in smart grid developments, capitalizing on decentralized, green power generation from, for example, solar panels.'

But Mettes is not the only person at Essent who is convinced that the future of energy lies in data. 'We are in essence a data company. The board has given me specific directives to focus on data initiatives and individual senior managers are strongly promoting data commercialization as a business driver.' But it is too early to speak of a corporate data strategy.

Mettes is realistic in her approach. Although she and the board are convinced that the future of the company depends heavily on the value of its data, she recognizes that Essent is currently in an explorative stage. Just as Eric Ries pointed out, Mettes realizes that innovation cannot be designed and planned and thus requires an iterative approach. 'Data is important, but we don't have a clear roadmap for data driven products or services. Innovation is not predictable. It is a process of trial and error. What is important is that we provide feedback to the organization on what we have learned.' With the focus of the company on financial performance, data innovation is like fighting a war on two fronts: Most successes do not contribute directly to the bottom line. And because data products are usually not directly related to the companies' core activities, employees often see them as an off-topic distraction rather than as an enabler for future value propositions. It makes for an environment where data driven innovation is a step-by-step exercise that requires constant attention from dedicated individuals. At Essent the increments are clearly recognizable. In 2011, the company made a strategic decision to create a customer insights system with the aim to collect as much customer data as possible to form a so-called 360-degree view of the customer.

The initiative is based on the early assumption that utility providers, in essence, are data driven organizations and that data can change commodity providers into value added service providers. Building on that thought, Essent was the first utility in market to introduce the 'e-Thermostat', which could be remotely controlled through an iPhone or iPad. Although strictly speaking not a data driven innovation, the e-Thermostat allowed Essent to monitor customer adoption of smart technology and make the first steps towards becoming a customer insights company. Close to a year later, Essent introduced 'e-Insight', a combination of 'smart' switch plugs that consumers can place between a wall socket and an electrical device and a smartphone app that shows exactly how much power that device consumes at any given time. Just like the e-Thermostat, the smart devices not only show the customer how much energy is being used, but they also allow Essent to give tailored advice on energy saving devices based on the profile of the individual customer that connected these 'e-Insight' products through their smartphones. Another small step, but a useful source of feedback. Roughly around the same time, Essent organized a hackathon for the development of mobile apps that supported and strengthened the functionality of the thermostat and switch plugs. And it founded the 'Open Data Collective', a group of eight corporations including Microsoft, Philips and Ricoh to co-create data driven solutions.

Marcelle Mettes underlines the importance of co-creation during the process. 'We quickly found out through trial and error that we couldn't develop all ideas and opportunities by ourselves. We simply do not have all of the required skills within Essent. We need partners. Universities, government, suppliers and grid companies. We create the right environment for innovation. Once successful, we provide the right acceleration mechanism, for instance by acting as the launching customer.' That is why Essent participates in and experiments with incubator programs, where rapid prototyping of new ideas is the focus. 'Our innovations currently have a tendency to focus within the energy-domain. That leads to short term added value, but also limits our long term options. This is why we seek partnerships outside our own business area. By combining data from our company with open data or with data from companies outside our domain, for instance mobile data, we can find new applications and business models.' The hackathon and Open Data Collective are mechanisms for this acceleration. They are aimed at discovering new business models and at carefully grooming them into viable products and services. 'Even when we find successful new opportunities, their short term turnover potential is often peanuts compared to existing business. So we are adding non-financial performance indicators for innovations, such as the capability to solve a customer problem or the scalability of a solution.'

Mettes acknowledges that the 'Commodity Swap' pattern is a likely scenario for energy companies such as Essent. 'Essent has started to transform its business to secure a leading position in the future. By developing and offering new data driven products and services that improve sustainable well-being, both at home and in the office. Data is a strategic asset in achieving that position. We carefully monitor all innovations within Essent on their focus and alignment to strategy. Through open innovation, strategic and commercial partnerships and governance of learnings we improve our position gradually. As we progress, senior management keeps close tabs on the developments and shapes its strategy accordingly. We don't have a roadmap, but we all know where we are headed.'

20 - Final Thoughts

This book started out describing events that happened not much more than ten years ago, a time when the Internet was changing the world. Now, that change has become the norm. But the process of change has not halted. Three major developments spawned from this process of change: the Connected Economy, the Internet of Things and Mobility. These changes combined have created both the opportunity and the demand for Data Driven Strategy.

Explaining these developments formed the key of the first section of this book. From there I showed typical business models that leverage the opportunities that data creates. After which I discussed the techniques and critical success factors for monetizing data. But the overarching goal of this book is not to lecture on what you should do. It is to inspire you to go out there and start working on your own Data Driven Strategy. Keep in mind that Data Driven Strategy is not a business solution in itself. It is a mechanism to help you to create new business solutions by unlocking the value that lies in data.

Data Driven Strategies do not grow overnight. At Apple, Nike, TomTom, Walmart, Samsung or Xiaomi success was not instant. It grew over time to form a formidable competitive advantage. On the road to success, highly motivated people tinkered and tuned. In Ries' words they 'pivoted and persevered'. Follow in their footsteps, go out and try. Find the building blocks. Play and discover. Share your ideas and discuss the opportunities with your team, with business partners and with your customers. Decide that you believe that data holds strategic value for your company. Create your Business Model Canvas, your own minimum viable data product. Test it with your customers. Co-create, learn and adapt. And more than anything: allow the data to spark your creativity.

21 - Get Involved

fter reading this book, I invite you to get involved in Data Driven Strategy. Feel free to connect on my blog, follow me on Twitter or join the LinkedIn Group on Data Driven Strategy. Share and discuss new business cases, opportunities, challenges and insights.

 http://www.datadrivenstrategy.net

 LinkedIn Group: Data Driven Strategy

 @avantspijker

22 - Index

23 - References

1   Google Inc., Google Investor Relations, February 8, 2012.
http://investor.google.com/financial/tables.html

2   Friedman, T. *The World is Flat*. (Macmillan, 2007)

3   Andreessen, M., *Why Software Is Eating The World*. WSJ.com. August 20, 2011.
http://online.wsj.com/news/articles/SB10001424053111903480904576512250915629460

4   United States Government. *Open Government Initiative*. 2013.
http://www.whitehouse.gov/open

5   Ashton, K., *That 'Internet of Things' Thing*. RFID Journal. June 22, 2009.
http://www.rfidjournal.com/articles/view?4986

6   Prahalad, C.K. and Ramaswamy, V., *The Future Of Competition: Co-Creating Unique Value With Customers*. (Harvard Business Review Press, 2004)

7   Soderquist, D., *The Wal-Mart Way: The Inside Story of the Success of the World's Largest Company*. (Thomas Nelson, 2005)

8   Qualman, E., *Socialnomics*. (Wiley, 2012)

9   MacManus, R., *Why HP Thinks Sensors Will Lead to The Next Big Wave of Computing*. HP.com May 27, 2010.
http://readwrite.com/2010/05/27/sensors_next_big_wave_of_computing#

10   Cisco Systems Inc., *The Internet of Things*. Cisco.com. June 3, 2011.
http://www.cisco.com/web/solutions/trends/iot/indepth.html

11   Oak Ridge National Laboratory, Sensorpedia.
        http://www.sensorpedia.com

12   Antorini, Y, Muñiz, Jr. A, and Askildsen, T., *Collaborating With Customer Communities: Lessons From the Lego Group.* MIT Sloan Management Review. March 20, 2012.
        http://sloanreview.mit.edu/article/collaborating-with-customer-communities-lessons-from-the-lego-group

13   Leber, J., *Why Samsung's Man in Silicon Valley Uses Apple Devices.* Technology Review. December 13, 2012.
        http://www.technologyreview.com/news/508306/why-samsungs-man-in-silicon-valley-uses-apple-devices

14   Gawer, A. and Cusmano, M. *Platform Leadership: How Intel, Microsoft, and Cisco Drive Industry Innovation.* (Harvard Business School Press, 2002)

15   Osterwalder, A. and Pigneur, Y., *Business Model Generation.* (John Wiley & Sons, 2010)

16   Anderson, C., *The Long Tail: Why the future of business is selling less of more.* (Hyperion, 2006)

17   Jones, R., *Barclays bank sell customer data.* The Guardian. June 24, 2013. http://www.theguardian.com/business/2013/jun/24/barclays-bank-sell-customer-data

18   JP Morgan Chase & Co., *Senior Product Manager - Intelligent Solutions.* LinkedIn.com. December 1, 2013.
        http://www.linkedin.com/jobs2/view/9932246

19   Crook, J., *Mint.com tops 10 million registered users.* Tech Crunch. August 29, 2012 http://techcrunch.com/2012/08/29/mint-com-tops-10-million-registered-users-70-come-from-mobile-vs-web/

20   Botsman, R., *Welcome to the new reputation economy.* Wired Magazine. August 20, 2012.
        http://www.wired.co.uk/magazine/archive/2012/09/features/welcome-to-the-new-reputation-economy

21   Ahmed, A. and Olander, S., *Velocity: The Seven New Laws for a World Gone Digital.* (Random House, 2012)

22   Covey, S.R., *Smart Trust.* (Simon & Schuster, 2012)

23   The Financial Brand. *Is The World Ready For Social Media Credit Scores?* The Financial Brand. August 14, 2012.
        http://thefinancialbrand.com/24733/social-media-credit-score/

24   Walmart, *Walmart Announces New Commitments to Dramatically Increase Energy Efficiency and Renewables* Walmart.com. April 15, 2013

http://news.walmart.com/news-archive/2013/04/15/walmart-announces-new-commitments-to-dramatically-increase-energy-efficiency-renewables

25   McKerracher, C. and Torriti, J., *Energy consumption feedback in perspective: integrating Australian data to meta-analyses on in-home displays*. Energy efficiency, Volume 6, 2013: 387 - 405.

26   Lucente, M, K Ting, G Fung, W Lee, and S. Hui., *A Taxonomy of Load Signatures for Single Phase Electric Applicances*. 2005 IEEE PESC (Power Electronics Specialist Conference). Recife, Brazil: IEEE, 2005.

27   Porter, Michael E., *Competitive Advantage: Creating and Sustaining Superior Performance*. (Simon & Schuster, 1985)

28   Monsanto Company. *Monsanto to Acquire The Climate Corporation, Combination to Provide Farmers with Broad Suite of Tools Offering Greater On-Farm Insights*. Monsato Newsroom. October 2, 2013. http://news.monsanto.com/press-release/corporate/monsanto-acquire-climate-corporation-combination-provide-farmers-broad-suite

29   Lichtenstein, N., *The Retail Revolution: How Wal-Mart Created a Brave New World of Business*. (Macmillan, 2009)

30   Dik, C., *Vandaag voor Morgen* TVA.nl May 18, 2010. http://www.tva.nl/upload/Albert%20Heijn_Vandaag%20voor%20morgen.pdf

31   Parolini, C., *The Value Net*. (John Wiley & Sons, 1999)

32   BBC, *Getty makes 35 million photos free to use*. BBC.com March 6, 2014 http://www.bbc.com/news/entertainment-arts-26463886

33   Ha, A., *Stipple Partners With Getty Images For Smarter In-Image Advertising*. Tech Crunch. June 21, 2013. http://techcrunch.com/2013/07/31/stipple-partners-with-getty-images

34   Collins, J. and Porras, J., *Built to Last: Successful Habits of Visionary Companies*. (Harper Business, 1994)

35   Wolverton, T., *Now showing: random DVD prices on Amazon*. C|Net. September 5, 2000. http://news.cnet.com/2100-1017-245326.html

36   IBM Corporation. *The IBM Data Governance Council Maturity Model: Building a roadmap for effective data governance*. IBM Data Governance Council, 2007.

37   Cranfield University. *Creating Resilient Supply Chains: A Practical Guide*. Centre for Logistics and Supply Chain Management, Cranfield School of Management, 2003, 21 - 29.

38   Wolf, M., *Connected Living Room Market Forecast: 2013-2017*. Edmunds: NextMarket Insights, 2013.

39   Hong, K., *China's Xiaomi sells 100,000 of its newest phone and in 86 seconds and 3,000 smart TV's in two minutes*. The Next Web, October 15, 2013. http://thenextweb.com/asia/2013/10/15/chinas-xiaomi-sells-100000-of-its-newest-phone-in-86-seconds-and-3000-smart-tvs-in-2-minutes/.

40   Gartner Inc., *Gartner Predicts 30 Percent of Businesses Will Be Monetizing Their Information Assets Directly by 2016*. Gartner.com. January 10, 2013. http://www.gartner.com/newsroom/id/2299315

41   McKenzie, H., *Lei Jun says Xiaomi's smart TV's are the ultimate Smartphone accessories*. Pando Daily, October 22, 2013. http://pando.com/2013/10/22/lei-jun-says-xiaomis-smart-tvs-are-the-ultimate-Smartphone-accessories/

42   US District Court, *Jane Doe vs. Netflix*. Wired.com, December 17, 2009. http://www.wired.com/images_blogs/threatlevel/2009/12/doe-v-netflix.pdf

43   Ohm, P., *Broken promises of privacy: Responding to the surprising failure of anonymization*. UCLA Law Review, 2010: 1701.

44   Taleb, N., *Antifragile: Things That Gain From Disorder*. (Random House, 2012)

45   Taleb, N., *Thriving on Disorder*. Nexus Institute. December 03, 2013. http://vimeo.com/81490200.

46   Huston, I and Sakkab, N., *P&G's New Innovation Model*. Harvard Business School, March 20, 2006. http://hbswk.hbs.edu/archive/5258.html.

47   Zuckerberg, M., *Mark Zuckerberg's letter to investors: The Hacker Way*. CNN Money February 01, 2012. http://money.cnn.com/2012/02/01/technology/zuckerberg_ipo_letter

48   Ries, E., *The Lean Startup: How Today's Entrepreneurs Use Continuous Innovation to Create Radically Successful Businesses*. (Viking, 2011)